GW00995281

Entering *into*
Promise *and* Inheritance

———

STEPHEN HILL

©2019

'Entering into Promise and Inheritance'
Written by Stephen Hill

Published by: Stephen Hill - Ancient Future 2019

Cover design & layout by Tom Carroll

ISBN: 978-0-473-49750-7

All rights reserved. No part of this publication may be reproduced, stored in a retrieval system, or transmitted in any form or by any means – for example, electronic, photocopy, recording - without the prior written permission of the publisher. The only exception is brief quotation in printed reviews.

All scripture quotations, unless otherwise indicated, are taken from the English Standard Version® (ESV®). All rights reserved.

This book is also available from Amazon: **www.amazon.com**

More resources can be found at:
www.ancientfuture.co.nz

ANCIENT
FUTURE

Dedicated to my dad, John Houston "Jack" Hill,
who went home on 26th August 2019.

CONTENTS

CONTENTS

PREFACE

In 2008 I had a profound experience of the Father's love; I was born again—*again*.

Before that I had frequent experiences of being hungry for God and since receiving that substance of love in my innermost being, I did not feel spiritual hunger again. I was filled with the substance of divine love and my hunger was satisfied.

In the last nine months, however, I have begun to experience spiritual hunger again; not so much hunger for God Himself but hunger to be an authentic expression of myself. Hunger for God *within me* to express Himself more powerfully *through me*.

I believe that many of us are on this journey. We are ready to take another step and push the boat out further on this journey in the Father's love.

This is a time for transition and a shifting of the season.

Over the last ten years I laid aside all of my desires to walk in spiritual power so that I would grow in love. I want to grow in love and then become transformed by love. But love needs *power*. Love is not insipid; love is *powerful*. If there is no power in love we cannot change the lives of others, and we cannot change situations. God has called His sons and daughters to change situations and that's really what's on my heart; that I would begin to move, that I would begin to take risks to explore the authority that I have as a son of the Father.

The time has now come to reintegrate things that we did before through the paradigm of orphan-spirited Christianity. Many of us (understandably) threw out the pentecostal/ charismatic baby with the bathwater. We set aside things like intercession, things like spiritual warfare because they were on a wrong foundation. But now that the foundation is set in place, I believe the time is coming (and is now here) to reintegrate these things into our lives *within this new reality of sonship.* If you know that you are a beloved son or daughter and you have an impulse from the heart to do something you did before in servanthood, it is probably not regression; it is most likely growth and progression.

It's time to explore. It's time to push out. It's time to flex our muscles. It is time to learn how to take faltering steps forward. It is time for some of us to progress from being babies to being toddlers.

This book is prophetic, intended to open up new possibilities, to vivify the heart to apprehend new realities, and to release hope into you, the reader.

I want to put words to what God is already doing. No one, not even the most anointed prophet, is ever ahead of what the Holy Spirit is working in the heart of any individual.

Prophetic ministry helps to reveal the mysteries that often cause us confusion. Prophetic revelation only puts words to what we are already experiencing in our spirits. The indwelling Spirit of the New Covenant is a more reliable and more accurate guide than prophecy. I hope and pray that this book contributes to that.

CHAPTER ONE

Exodus, Transition, And Entry

Are you moving or are you stuck? Have you experienced some powerful move of God in your life but somehow things now seem to be a bit humdrum? Are you hungry for the next move of God? Are you wondering when, or even if, God is going to move again? If you recognise these feelings then this book may be for you.

It has often been pointed out that those who were leaders in the previous move of God are the ones who are most resistant to the next move of God. That is sad but it doesn't always have to be this way. There will be a move of God that will be the ultimate move, the final move, and no more moves will be needed because we will be in a place of rest, of being united with Him in His environment of perfected love. That is the promise and it is for everyone. It is to be activated in every member of the Body of Christ and in all creation.

We are coming out of slavery, moving through transition and entering into promise. God is bringing us into our inheritance. But the way forward is not through the methods we have known in the past. We are often so fixated on how God moved in the past that we cannot discern what He is doing *today* and, as a result, we miss out on the glorious future.

I want to take a well known biblical narrative to communicate this. It is the story of the children of Israel coming out of Egypt and going through the wilderness into the promised land. This story has caught the imagination of movie makers. The epic *The Ten Commandments* (1956) starring Charlton Heston, the animated film, *The Prince of Egypt* (1998) and the more recent *Exodus: Gods and Kings* (2014) are worth watching to stimulate our imaginations. I want to use this story from the Old Testament as a metaphor for what happens in our spiritual experience. My graphic below sets out what it looks like:

EGYPT	WILDERNESS	PROMISED LAND
SLAVERY	TRANSITION	FREEDOM
FEAR		PERFECT LOVE
ORPHANNESS		SONSHIP
INSECURITY		IDENTITY
LACK OF COMFORT		FULNESS OF COMFORT
NO IDENTITY		COMPLETE IDENTITY
FIGLEAVES / FALSE SELF		CHRISTLIKE-NESS/ TRUE SELF

We are transitioning from the left-hand side of my graphic over to the right-hand side. In the middle is the unavoidable wilderness. We may balk at the wilderness but it is necessary. We need to have confidence that our Father and our Lord Jesus Christ, by the Holy Spirit, are fully committed to leading us through the desert experience to the land of fulfilment, promise and inheritance. The experience of the Passover and the Red Sea demonstrates, if nothing else, the absolute and sovereign control of God. He shows up in power to demonstrate who He is to the Egyptians. He splits the Red Sea and then shows up in the pillar of cloud and fire. Through the Exodus and the wilderness the supernatural intervention of God is very evident.

God is never caught off guard nor is He unprepared for anything. It is we who need to understand what He is doing. God is constantly at work, loving us and bringing us deeper and deeper into His love. He is also working so that He will be able to express His love through us. God is liberating us from the most fundamental symptom of our separation from Him; He is liberating us *from* fear. He is liberating us *into* His perfect love.

CHAPTER TWO

What Is Our Inheritance And Destiny?

Inheritance and destiny are very popular concepts in contemporary Christianity. The idea of 'destiny' or 'inheritance' can certainly put bums on seats, no doubt about that!

But what, exactly, is our inheritance? How are we to understand this idea of 'destiny'?

First and foremost, above everything else, our destiny is to be like Christ. The Holy Spirit will never lead us into anything other than Christlikeness. The high point of success in the Christian life is martyrdom, either by means of dying or by daily living. We cannot experience true Christianity by bypassing the cross. The cross has put an end to any orphan agenda in order to release the blessing of the Father.

Our greatest inheritance is not necessarily to have what the world defines as a successful life. I have no doubt that God wants the best for His children; for them to be healthy, happy and fulfilled. God wants to prosper us. Some churches have as their motto, '*Your Best Life*' but your 'best life' as a Christian may entail being a martyr. How about literal martyrdom as your inheritance? We need a Christianity like the martyrs had, a love stronger than death. Never forget that the high point of the Christian life could involve martyrdom.

Above all else, our inheritance and promise is to be like His Son. God is totally focused on this. Our inheritance is to live in Christ, to be in union with Him.

More specifically, however, your inheritance is the state where God can express Himself through you. That means you need to become who you really are, uniquely individual. You don't need to suppress your creativity and join an institution or a programme; that is not how the Kingdom of God works. The Kingdom of God is a symphony of many different expressions. Your inheritance will be your own expression, joined with others, and anointed by divine love and power. The love of God is producing this and bringing it forth. That is our destination.

Believe it or not, it takes a lot to stop us getting to the destination. God is very involved and committed to helping us become free. Too many preachers and leaders are quick to put heavy burdens of guilt on people and insinuate that the people are sinful, lazy and not spiritually motivated. This is not true. I believe that the vast, vast majority of people who call themselves Christian (maybe even those who do not) have hearts that *really want* union with God and likeness to Jesus. That is not the real issue. What stops us is not our 'naughtiness.' I believe our problem is more that we do not understand the spiritual processes of how God works in our lives.

WE ARE GOD'S INHERITANCE

We are entering into the promised land that God has prepared for us. Bit by bit we are being cajoled through the wilderness and towards our inheritance.

But do you realise that *God* has an inheritance *too*? Do you realise that God Himself is on a journey towards a land that He has promised Himself?

And what is God's inheritance? God's inheritance is you and I; *we* are the land of God's inheritance. God has a dream home; it is us, His set-apart ones (Ephesians 1:18) God wants to live in us, individually and corporately. He wants to renovate us, decorate us according to His imagining and dreaming. Jesus said, "If anyone loves Me, he will keep My word. My Father will love him, and We will come to him and make Our home with him." (John 14:23)

God wants to relax and be at home within us; He wants to put His feet up and kick off His shoes. And He wants to stay and never leave.

It goes without saying that God doesn't need to come out of slavery. He was never in bondage to anything. But He has to deal with a few giants of false beliefs *in us* so that He can come and fully inhabit us. God Himself wants to live and expand, be planted and blossom within humans. Believe this now! Believe that God is seeping into you, rushing into you. Close your eyes right now and feel it; open your heart to it and believe it. Believe that God is entering more fully into you, His promised land.

This is true on an individual level. It is also true on a corporate level. The whole Body of Christ is a land of promise that God wishes to completely live in and fill.

Has God entered *His* promised land yet? Has God entered fully into *His* rest yet? It is surely coming. He is descending into our humanity to rest there. The Trinity wants to relax within you and have more freedom to express the personality of God.

God is not afraid of the giants in the land. You need to see your issues as God sees them. It is a question of belief. The power of condemnation makes you think that your stuff is a 'giant' but, in reality, it is insignificant to God. If we could only see that God is entering us, and dismiss our unworthiness as a lie, then we would experience God within us much more easily.

The dominion of God's love is to come within us, on earth as it is in heaven. Every time I go through difficulties in life I have massive hope because I see that God is pushing deeper into His inheritance. If something is causing me discomfort, I see it as God cleaning out a room, moving furniture, dumping old rubbish, scrubbing the floor, rewiring the electrics. When we see it this way, it puts our struggles into a much more hopeful light. Instead of coming under condemnation and doubt, I now see it as God establishing His home within me, so that He can more fully express Himself through the unique vessel that is me.

CHAPTER THREE

What Stops Us Entering Into Inheritance?

There are two major stumbling blocks that stop us entering into promise. It takes a paradigm shift to identify and overcome them because they are deeply ingrained in our Christian worldview and psyche.

1. THE BLUEPRINT OF OUR DESTINY IS IN OUR HUMANITY

The first, vitally important, thing to understand is this:

Your destiny is already hardwired into your humanity.

Destiny, inheritance, and promise are not issues of salvation; they are issues of *redemption* to what we have been created for in the first place. This is where religion, among other influences, has misled us. We have not realised the full meaning of redemption. Redemption means to buy back that which was previously owned. God previously owned us, loved us, and created us *as humans*. He redeemed us to be fully human before Him again. We have not even begun to scratch the surface of what God intended for us as fully human.

When God does His work in our lives, it is to remove the masks, the false identities that are nothing more than fig leaves. We do not make gains spiritually by doing more or by addition; we make gains (at least, initially) by *subtraction*. The false needs to be subtracted until God gets to the ground of our being, to the core of who we are. He then builds, adds and multiplies from there!

What you will emerge into is already hardwired into your humanity.

In this ministry of the Father's love, God is stripping away false identities (fig leaves) to reveal our true selves. The true self is much bigger, in reality, than the false self. **We are being 'reduced' to something bigger.** We are being undressed to our original nakedness—*without any shame*. Who you really are is an identity unaffected by shame. The true you has intrinsic significance.

Your inheritance fits you like a glove. But it doesn't fit the false you; it fits the *real* you…perfectly. If you are caught in religion and shame, if you are running from who you really are, you will never discover your destiny.

Our destiny doesn't come through salvation; it comes through *creation*. Contrary to what many Evangelical Christians assume, salvation is *not* the beginning. Our chosenness before creation is the beginning (Ephesians 1).

Many think that God reluctantly rescues us from

absolute depravity but He doesn't really love us. He is forced to honour a covenant because it is a legal agreement. Even lines of worship songs, such as "…and I don't deserve it…" (talking about the love of God) are rooted in a shame-based theology. The thing is, we *do* deserve the love of God because we were created by Love Itself *to be loved*. We were predestined to be "…holy and blameless before Him in love." (Ephesians 1:4) God saw you before the foundation of the world and purposed to redeem you into being a manifestation of His loving design for your life.

A lot of our Western Christianity has been influenced by Greek philosophy rather than a Biblical (Hebraic) worldview. Someone has said that the Church, historically, has been more influenced by Plato than Jesus. Put simply, Plato taught that the human body was at worst evil and at best a prison. This is not the way the Hebrews thought. Christianity is not about escaping from our humanness; it is about accepting and celebrating that our humanness, weak and flawed though it may be, is the clay pot that the treasure is kept in (2 Corinthians 4:7).

James Jordan has said that anyone who is called to be a preacher will invariably have a lifelong inbuilt love of words and language. The person called to be a preacher is always searching for the right language to articulate what the Spirit of God is saying. If you don't love words, you are most likely *not* called to be a speaker. A sudden interest and desire for words and communication is not going to be downloaded into you in a charismatic experience. The love of words will be there and will have been instilled in you naturally from early childhood; it will be hardwired into you from a very young age. This may burst your bubble but it should also liberate you.

As far back as I can remember, I was fascinated with words, with stories. I loved reading books about adventure, heroism, and epic journeys. As a child, it wasn't long before I discovered that this was problematic. You see, I was brought up in an environment which was very religious and legalistic and which frowned upon the arts and literature. Because my father disapproved of me reading these 'worldly' novels, I was forced to hide books under the floorboards in my bedroom. It took me a long time to discover that my love for stories had actually been given to me by my heavenly Father.

Paul, the apostle, stated in his letter to the community in Galatia, that God had chosen and set him apart 'from his mother's womb.' His calling was hardwired into him as an integral part of God's creation. This is not unique to Paul. We are *all* called from our mother's womb; life is about discovering who we are as God has originally created us.

This is not to say that spiritual ministry works through natural talent. Because you are naturally gifted or have talent, it does not mean that the Spirit of God has anointed you. But spiritual anointing *does flow* like electricity through the conduit of your unique human personality. The work of the Spirit in our lives is to help us uncover our true self and discover who we are called to be.

I have discovered things that my Creator has hardwired into me that I had no idea were part of my unique personality. I was not given the opportunity to express them in my childhood, but they were in my personality while I was in my mother's womb. As we get liberated from judgments about ourselves, we will find that creative expression begins to flow once again in us. This is not a new thing; it is, rather, an unveiling of the glorious and creative being that God already sees you to be. God sees you in a way that your parents, no matter how good they have been, can *never* see.

One of the major reasons why we cannot enter into promise and destiny is because we have been deceived into thinking that promise and destiny involve us moving away from, not closer to, our true selves. The opposite is true. The promise and the inheritance is actually to be Christ *in you*. (Colossians 1:27) It is the integration of the divine within the human and the synthesis of Jesus being completely true to Himself and you completely true to yourself. Jesus cannot be true to Himself in you when you are not true to yourself. He is 'truth' so He can only express Himself with anointing in reality.

When the integration of Jesus and you, of heaven and earth happens, you will begin to see promise erupting all around you.

2. ENTRY INTO THE LAND IS A DIFFERENT PROCESS THAN EXODUS FROM EGYPT

The second major realisation that needs to occur, if we are going to move out of the wilderness phase into promise, inheritance and destiny, is this:

Entry is a different process than Exodus

We are stuck because we expect it to happen in the same way as our exodus from slavery—but it doesn't!

Everyone is always longing for 'revival.' It is like a mirage in the desert, always ahead of us but we are never able to actually reach it. This is a huge problem in the contemporary Church. We always expect that the next move of God will happen just like the previous one.

When the Israelites came out of Egypt, all they had to do was follow Moses. Moses was their connection to God. The people, who had lived in the culture of Egypt for 430 years according to Exodus 12:40, had no idea of who Yahweh was. Only Moses carried the revelation of a Voice that spoke from the burning bush as "I AM THAT I AM, the God of Abraham, the God of Isaac, the God of Jacob." Moses was God's representative to the people; it was indisputably proved by the signs and wonders worked through him. God gave Moses instructions, communicating regularly and personally to him. And Moses carried a big stick with magical powers!

In awe of Moses and the God he represented, the Israelites followed him toward the Red Sea. They themselves had no functioning relationship with this Deliverer-God. But that was to change; in the wilderness they were to get an unveiling of who this God really is.

My point here is this: It was through Moses that the Exodus took place. When it comes to entering the Promised Land, however, there is a different requirement and a different sequence of events.

The next move of God will not happen in the same way as the last move of God. This is a universal principle. God does not move in the same way twice. But, this has extra significance because what God is doing now is unprecedented in a *unique* way.

There is a mega-shift happening in the understanding and experience of Christianity. The method of delivering the Good News is changing. An abundance of seminars and conferences is not sufficient to reach a groaning creation with the Gospel.

We need to understand that *almost every* move of God, throughout the long history of the Church, have been movements of leading the Church *out of Egypt*. Generally speaking, the Church does not know how to enter the

Promised Land. There have been movements of the Spirit which have shown something of what the Promised Land is like, but they have been largely missed because everyone was mesmerised by what God did to release us from bondage *in the past.*

I say it again: When the children of Israel came out of Egypt they didn't have to rely on their own faith. They put their faith in their saviour, Moses. Moses had delivered them through a display of signs and wonders. It was Moses who faced down Pharaoh and demanded the release of the Israelites. It was Moses who called down the power of God to force a way out of Egypt. He alone exercised the faith for supernatural breakthrough. He wielded his staff and the Israelites followed him. They didn't know everything that was going on but they were persuaded that Moses was their deliverer and rescuer. The children of Israel didn't need to hear from God; Moses heard from God and they obeyed him. He stretched out his staff, touched the Red Sea and it parted, letting them through. The Egyptian army was engulfed as the waters rushed together again.

When we come out of slavery, we only have enough faith to open our hearts to the anointed minister. We place faith outside of ourselves in another, and ultimately in our Saviour, Jesus. Many Pentecostals and Charismatics have had powerful experiences of the Holy Spirit in anointed meetings. Many have been called out and prophesied over, many have experienced the supernatural touch of God in

places like Toronto, Pensacola, Sunderland, Lakeland—
the list goes on. These experiences have propelled us out
of slavery but what happens then? We transition into wilderness and begin to wander round and round. We cannot
enter promise; we are frustrated because the prophetic
promises over us remain unfulfilled. Why is this?

We cannot enter promise because we have an expectation that entry into the promised land happens in the same
way that we were delivered from slavery—but it doesn't!
Entry into the land has a very different process than exodus
from Egypt.

Many people pray, "Lord, do it again," but will the
Lord do it the same way? Will our past experiences be
repeated? More than likely they won't. This may be why we
are stuck in a holding pattern, never actually getting into
our inheritance.

Moses told the people to stand still and witness God's
salvation (Exodus 14:13,14) but when it comes to Joshua, *he*
needs to arise and make a movement. (Joshua 1:2) This is
the difference that we need to be aware of. The time comes
when we need to make a movement towards the place where
we are meant to be.

If you are looking for a saviour to stretch out a staff and
propel you into promise and destiny, you will be looking
a long time because it won't happen. Many Christians are
hovering in trepidation on the banks of the Jordan hanging

out for a Red Sea experience which will never come. But God is very confident. He wants to show us how to transition into all that He has purposed for us.

CHAPTER FOUR

How Did We End Up In Egypt?

Before I say any more, let me set a context. How did the children of Israel arrive at the point of needing to be rescued from Egypt?

It begins back in Genesis. God connected with a man called Abraham and promised him that his offspring would be a vehicle of blessing for the nations. Abraham, Isaac, then Jacob, all ventured with God.

We then pick up the story in Genesis 37 and the following chapters, where we read about Jacob's son named Joseph. The old man, Jacob, blatantly favoured this boy, Joseph, to the annoyance and growing jealousy of the brothers. Joseph knew that favour was upon him. He was very aware of his charisma; he really rubbed it into his brothers, and even into his father and mother. This culminated in the brothers throwing Joseph into a pit, then selling him to a camel caravan of merchants on their way to Egypt.

Joseph found himself in Egypt. Through a number of twist and turns he eventually found himself in a place of significant favour and success. He became vizier (prime minister) of Egypt, second in command to the king. Circumstances reconnected Joseph to his brothers and his aged father found joy again that, after all, his beloved son was not dead but alive and living in Egypt.

Joseph used his influence to bring his family out of the famine of Canaan to the province of Goshen. They were under Joseph's patronage, they were well looked after and they prospered.

That is a thumbnail sketch of how they ended up in Egypt.

Jump forward four centuries.[1] We pick up the narrative at the beginning of Exodus. Dark clouds had begun to gather on the horizon. The political climate was beginning to shift, to the absolute detriment of the children of Israel.

There was a pharaoh on the Egyptian throne "who did not know Joseph." (Exodus 1:8) He did not recognise the dignity that Joseph's name carried in Egypt. This new king took umbrage against the Hebrews. He started by discriminating against them, then upped the ante by openly intimidating them. Within a number of generations, they went from prosperity and favour to slavery and fear. Their identity was systematically obliterated. In Egypt, the children of Israel lost all sense of being owned and called by God. They effectively became orphans, without identity or history.

---

1. According to Exodus 12: 40 the Israelites were in Egypt for 430 years.

They lost the sense of chosenness they had as descendants of Abraham, Isaac and Jacob. They were reduced to scrabbling for food and slaving in the brickyards under the whip of the slavemasters.

I want to propose that the same thing has happened to us. We were created to be God's children, prospering under His love. A series of disasters, beginning with the Fall of the first humans and their expulsion from the Garden, have ultimately brought us into slavery. We are not who we should be; we are not the glorious and wonderful creation that God sees and has planned for us to be. We need to be rescued and set free.

Slaving In
The Brickyards

The Despot of Egypt, the Pharaoh, oppressed the people of Israel:

> *"Therefore they set taskmasters over them to afflict them with heavy burdens. They built for Pharaoh store cities, Pithom and Raamses. But the more they were oppressed the more they multiplied and the more they spread abroad. And the Egyptians were in dread of the people of Israel. So they ruthlessly made the people of Israel work as slave and made their lives bitter with hard service, in mortar and brick, and in all kinds of work in the field. In all their work they ruthlessly made them work as slaves"* — EXODUS 1:11-14

Then Pharaoh tightened the screws on the Hebrew slaves:

> *"The same day Pharaoh commanded the taskmasters of the people and their foremen, 'You shall no longer give the people straw to*

> *make bricks, as in the past; let them go and*
> *gather straw for themselves. But the number*
> *of bricks that they made in the past you shall*
> *impose on them, you shall by no means reduce*
> *it, for they are idle.'"* — EXODUS 5:8,9

This is exactly what the world system does to us. Once we were identified as the favoured children of God, but we have ended up completely absorbed within the orphan system. The Cosmic Pharaoh (Satan in his many manifestations) has systematically practiced his form of ethnic cleansing on humanity to rob the whole human race of their true identity as the Father's children.

Some of us have tried to please God by being good and always doing what we were told. We tried to please a perceived 'God' who we thought to be a hard taskmaster. We found ourselves sucked deeper and deeper into the religious machine, pumping out bricks of ministry programmes, Christian activity, or self-denial by willpower.

This was *me*. I drove a wedge between the spiritual and the secular, suppressing the legitimate needs of my human heart. I had gone through some crises in my life, hurting myself and others because I was so out of touch with my true self. I wasn't in any way an integrated person.

Around 2005, my energy began to wane significantly. I noticed that it was taking more and more effort to be able to feed my 'zeal' for God. I was perplexed then but I now know what was happening. The straw which I needed to make the bricks had been taken away. Unknown to me at the time, I had to go out and find my own straw!

At the end of 2007 my brick-making effort could no longer handle it. The slave driver dealt me a blow with his whip and I collapsed. The Stephen Hill who could produce bricks in the factory of orphanness never rose again. I am permanently exhausted with a 'Christianity' that requires me to trot out products on the assembly line. The ministry machine gobbled me up and spat me out like mincemeat. In 2007, I finally collapsed and, with a shock, realised that my true condition was that of a slave.

You may not identify with my experience. Many don't. You may have been caught up in that other machine, the alternative manifestation of the brickyard. You may be caught by the lure of the secular world, the culture of the internet, of fashionable trends. You may be caught by addictions to the *bad* side of the Tree of Knowledge—sex, drugs, rock 'n roll!

The 'bad' side of the Tree of Knowledge is more obvious. The pressure of the world through celebrity culture and social media is relentless, particularly on young people. This is a culture of who can get laid, who can hold their drink, who drives the flashiest car. This is the culture of political correctness, of sexual fluidity, of the blurring of gender, of relentless peer pressure.

This is also a brickyard. You will find, as age lines your

face and you begin to sag, that you have to work harder to keep up with everyone else. The straw (energy) to produce the goods is taken away and you have to work harder with less resources.

The Orphan system (in its religious and secular manifestations) has us under slavery to its means of production. Initially it provides us with the means to keep the system going (youth, energy, zeal, enthusiasm, guilt, condemnation, dreams, media) At a certain time in life the means to sustain our productivity are taken away. This is called disillusionment and burnout.

Now, listen to me: Don't leave your job because you sometimes feel like a slave, and you have to work on a beautiful sunny day when you would rather be at the beach or drinking cocktails by the pool. That is not what I am advocating at all. I am talking about a deeper reality that we are caught in because of our orphan condition. This is what the Tree of Knowledge does to us.

On the one side of the Tree of Knowledge, we end up responding to every altar call. We volunteer for more and more programmes which are offered. One ministry internship is not enough; we have to attend every internship offered by all the current ministries. On the *other* side it is another drink, or a stronger drug, or more debt incurred to keep up with the Joneses, whether they live next door or in the pages of Hello magazine.

In the Tree of the Knowledge of Good and Evil, we are in a vicious cycle, never able to please God, never able to attain Christlikeness, never finding our destiny. Religion is the industry of making fig leaves to cover up our perceived shame. Religion apparently offers us an escape ladder from our base humanness so that we can somehow leap up to God. The truth is the opposite; God wants to come and indwell our humanity, to fill the dirt with glory-gold.

The bottom line is this: we all find ourselves in the same place; we have to keep producing something to keep life going. I am sure that you, the readers of this book, recognise that your ability to be productive is being taken away from you. No matter how hard you try, your energy is being sapped, and the altar call won't fix it.

Here we are, in Egypt, with no real identity, exhausted under the relentless heat of the sun beating down on our raw and lacerated backs…

C H A P T E R   S I X

Free At Last!

The brickyards are relentless but there is hope! God raised up a saviour to deliver Israel. Moses, the erstwhile 'Prince of Egypt' reappeared from a forty-year exile. He confronted Pharaoh, rescued the Israelites and led them out of bondage into the desert. He embarked them on a journey towards their true identity in God. In the wilderness the Ten Commandments were given as a founding constitution of a fledgling nation, showing them what Yahweh was like, unique among the panoply of the gods.

We are set free from the tyranny of the orphan system and we are set free to walk into a growing connection with God, to learn to hear His voice in the wilderness, to learn to worship Him without the trappings of orphan culture or doctrine.

We can be set free from a lot of what gave us our old identity as slaves. In the orphan world our identity comes from what we do, not from who we are. Having an identity which comes from a function (no matter how sophisticated the function) is still the identity of a slave. When we are set free from this we are very disorientated, having been stripped of our role, our function, our task (which was killing us anyway) but we are left wondering, "What next?" We cannot yet make decisions for ourselves; we still need to be told what to do. We have been set free from slavery but we are not yet free *in freedom*. (Galatians 5:1)

The experience of being set free cannot be achieved without some form of supernatural sign and wonder. This may not necessarily be something outwardly spectacular. It may be receiving a life-altering revelation that shakes the foundations of the religious edifice. It may be experienced as deep comfort and peace flooding through the heart that takes your insecurity away. If you have not been shaken and led through the 'night' and through a 'Red Sea' (either by crisis or by process) I would lovingly challenge you to look to see if you have really received a paradigm-shifting revelation. Ask the Spirit to deepen the realisation that your condition is an orphan condition, and to show you that you need to be set free from the bondage of orphanness by encountering the Father.

CHAPTER SEVEN

Entering
The Wilderness

Once we have crossed the Red Sea and escaped from our slavery we are faced with the wilderness. We are liberated from the harassment of slavery and escape the prison of orphan spirited Christianity. The question then arises, "What *now*? Where do we go *now*?" We are led into the wilderness!

The wilderness is a culture shock but it is essential for transition. The desert is a place for getting rid of the culture of slavery. It is one thing to take us out of Egypt; it is something else to take Egypt out of us. In the desert, the influences and baggage of orphan-hearted life drop away. That can be very uncomfortable. As soon as we enter the wilderness we have a sense of relief that the 'Egyptians' are no longer breathing down our neck, but we are also disorientated.

Many people find themselves in a wilderness where they have little to help them. Going to church has lost its appeal. There is no motivation for disciplines such as 'quiet times' or systematic Bible reading. We find this unsettling. Feelings of confusion and condemnation bite at our heels and we try to restart the old engine of will-driven spirituality. The wilderness is a relief from slavery, but then boredom kicks in and we think, "At least we knew what to do when the slave-drivers were over us." The people of Israel hankered after Egypt when things got challenging in the wilderness. (Numbers 11) While they were in Egypt they didn't have to use any initiative or creativity. All they had to do was follow the programme set out for them by their masters and woe betide if they didn't do it.

In servant-hearted Christianity we lack permission to say, 'No.' There is no permission to take a break, to put programmes on the shelf, or even abandon activity altogether. In the wilderness, however, the tyranny of fruitless activity is absent. The wilderness can be a very boring place for our flesh but it can be enjoyable too. When I went to the wilderness of Great Barrier Island, New Zealand for three months in 2008, it became the most cathartic experience I have ever had. No shopping malls, no Netflix, very restricted internet. Three months of little external stimulation but I was able to slow down enough to transition through the deep transformation that God was working in me.

Wilderness time does not have to be arduous. It can be enjoyable. Maybe it is time to take up travelling or rediscover an old hobby. Maybe it is the season to enjoy a normal job. There is virtually no religious stimulation in our spiritual wilderness. We are freed up from distraction to look inwards. This can be emotional hell but we discover heaven. The wilderness is a place of boredom for a while but then we discover an unprecedented wellspring of creativity bubbling up. This creativity is a foretaste of our destiny.

The contemporary Church has largely lost this sense of need for a desert and wilderness experience. There is scant understanding of the natural rhythms of spiritual life. Autumn and winter seasons in the Spirit become 'issues of pastoral concern.' There needs to be a return to the ancient ways, the rhythm of the seasons, a deeper spirituality. The experience of the desert is an integral part of that.

As we go through the wilderness we discover the formation of a new identity. They hadn't journeyed far before they reached Mount Sinai, the place where they received the Ten Commandments carved on two tablets of stone. The Ten Commandments and the subsequent Law had a number of different purposes but what I wish to highlight here is that they formed a new identity for a people who had been nothing more than slaves. The Ten Commandments was the foundational document, a constitution, for a new nation. God saw these people for who they really were, and the giving of the Law was intended to create an identity for them, to give them values based upon some knowledge of who this God, the God of their fathers, was.

The Law created a shape by saying; "No! You cannot do these things because they mess with your identity!"

Whatever the Law forbade was destructive to their identity anyway. As the Law was followed, it was intended to result in greater self-confidence and health. That was the intention of God.

In the wilderness we begin to get a revelation of the Law of the Spirit of Life in Christ Jesus, setting us free from the law of sin and death.

The exodus and the wilderness are times of supernatural display and supernatural encounter. Supernatural experience is normal as we are freed from slavery and as we enter into the wilderness. As we leave Egypt and transition through the wilderness, the underlying and dominant revelation is 'God *for* us.'

But the Land of Promise and Inheritance has a *different* revelation. When we get to the Land of Promise and Inheritance, the revelation will be "Christ *in* us" (Colossians 1:27).

ELEVEN DAYS OR FORTY YEARS?

There is a tremendous battle of faith in the wilderness. A lot of problems arise because we do not transition quickly enough. What was meant to be a journey of only eleven days for the Israelites took forty years!

God's plan for our transition from slavery and fear to love and Christlikeness is not meant to be as long as we fear. It should only take the proverbial eleven days to transition from orphanness to sonship. Transition is a process but it doesn't have to be arduous if we are willing to open our hearts enough to what the Spirit wants to accomplish in us:

Within eleven days of leaving Mount Horeb (Sinai) they came to a point of being able to cross over into the Promised Land, to Kadesh-barnea. The distance between those two points is only eleven days journey. (Deuteronomy 1:2) From that vantage point they sent spies into the land who returned with a largely negative report. Only two of the spies brought back a positive report of a good land, an abundant land of massive fertility. The other ten spies admitted that it was a good land but the obstacles were too big. They had a very low concept of who they were in comparison to the occupants of the land:

> *"We came to the land to which you sent us. It flows with milk and honey, and this is its fruit. However, the people who dwell in the land are strong, and the cities are fortified and very large. And besides, we saw the descendants of Anak there. The Amalekites dwell in the land of the Negeb. The Hittites, the Jebusites, and the Amorites dwell in the hill country. And the Canaanites dwell by the sea, and along the Jordan."* — Numbers 13:27-29

Caleb tried to put his perspective of faith across to the people, without success:

*"But Caleb quieted the people before Moses
and said, "Let us go up at once and occupy it,
for we are well able to overcome it." Then the
men who had gone up with him said, "We are
not able to go up against the people, for they
are stronger than we are." So they brought to
the people of Israel a bad report of the land
that they had spied out, saying, "The land,
through which we have gone to spy it out, is a
land that devours its inhabitants, and all the
people that we saw in it are of great height.
And there we saw the Nephilim (the sons of
Anak, who come from the Nephilim), and we
seemed to ourselves like grasshoppers, and so
we seemed to them." —* NUMBERS 13:30-33

The people believed the negativity of the ten spies. They
didn't have the faith to enter in when God wanted them
to enter into their possession. So they turned back and
continued to go round and round the wilderness for *forty*
years. The book of Hebrews reports, tragically, that not
one of the original group (apart from Joshua and Caleb)
who left Egypt actually entered the Land of Promise.
(Hebrews 3:16-19)

The journey from fear into love, from orphanness to
sonship is only meant to be a journey of eleven days. Can
you believe that? By the grace of God, I am here to help
you cut your transition from forty years to a much shorter

period. I believe that this book will help us transition a lot quicker than otherwise we would. If we can identify some of the reasons why they could not enter their inheritance, maybe it will help us enter ours.

As the wilderness causes the trappings of slavery and fear to fall away from us, we are learning to follow our hearts more. We are beginning to break free, bit by bit, from the obligations of addiction, and from doing things to earn brownie points with God. We are gradually getting to know who God really is, and beginning, *just beginning*, to worship Him in spirit and in truth, as *Father*. Oftentimes it seems like one step forward and two steps back. But the overall progression is still in a positive direction towards knowing who our Father really is.

Positioned To Enter Into Promise

After Exodus and the journey through the wilderness we come to the book of Joshua. Israel has the opportunity now to cross over the Jordan and enter in the land. The bones of the original escapees from Egypt are strewn in the wilderness. Joshua begins:

> *"After the death of Moses the servant of the LORD, the LORD said to Joshua the son of Nun, Moses' assistant, 'Moses my servant is dead. Now therefore arise, go over this Jordan, you and all this people, into the land that I am giving to them…'"* — JOSHUA 1:1,2

At the very beginning of Joshua we have the death of the servant and the sending of the son. Servanthood has no inheritance. The inheritance is only for sonship.

We can never enter promise and inheritance while we still adhere to the core identity of a servant. It is only when our self-belief shifts into the fact that we are *sons* that we can begin to appropriate the promised destiny. Only when we come into the life of sonship (through the continual experiencing of the Father loving us) does the possibility arise of entering into our inheritance. The servant has to die in order for the son to emerge.

You must come to the realisation that no matter how powerful your Christianity has been; if it merely identifies itself with obeying God as a commander, then *it needs to die* before you can enter into promise. Why? Because Christianity is not about being a servant. Christianity is about being *a son*.

Sons do serve but it is not their core identity. My core identity is not as a servant in the Kingdom of God. My foundational reality is that I am a son in the Father's family. My Papa is a King and He has a vast, ever-expanding kingdom. The Royal Family serve the interests of the Crown, but they have a vastly different sense of identity because they know their family heritage. As a son of the Heavenly Royal Family I serve *from* blessing, not to earn it. Sons serve out of the overflow of the Father's love, synergised with the Father's interests, aligned with the Father's vision and values. Our service as sons is as effective as our connection with the heart of the Father.

Let me give an illustration. A billionaire businessman has a very successful corporation. He has a son who has little sense of responsibility, who just lives to party, who takes advantage of having been born with the silver spoon in his mouth. The father has tried to include the son in the business but the son is not in the least interested.

But the billionaire business magnate has a very dedicated executive who acts as his 'right-hand' in running the business empire. This employee is extremely competent and trustworthy.

When the owner dies, who will inherit the business empire and the assets? Generally speaking, it won't be the employee. The *son* will inherit; and in many cases the son or daughter who inherits the business rises to the responsibility and is able to shoulder it.

There may be a well-loved and deeply respected king. He is wise and rules with a benevolent sceptre over his people. His courtiers are faithful and competent. He has an heir but the prince is a playboy, only interested in enjoying himself. But who is the heir to the throne? It is not the courtier or the official. It is the prince. Inheritance flows to sons.

The purpose of our wilderness journey is to give enough time for the servant to die and the son to come forth. We have to come to a realisation that no matter how powerful it was, the Christianity that identifies itself as merely *serving* God has to die in order to enter into promise because *promise only comes to sonship.*

This is what is happening in our lives. The servant, the highly anointed servant who was used mightily in leadership, is dying in the wilderness. The powerful and gifted servant needs to die so that God can say to the son "Arise!" and begin to move forward.

Many Christians are expecting to inherit the promise through following the path of anointed servanthood. We cry out with anguished longing, "More, Lord!" If anointing is poured upon servanthood it *still* won't inherit. A son with a dribble of anointing will inherit more than a servant who is saturated with anointing.

THE EMERGENCE OF THE BRIDE

Entering the inheritance and the promise is not only for us as *individuals*. The Church *corporately* is moving toward a Promised Land. God is calling forth the Body of Christ into her identity and into the fulness of who she is intended to be. The Body of Christ is a spiritual entity comprised of many members, and *we* are the members. For many years I could see that God wanted to bring forth the Body of Christ. I began to work for this vision with so much zeal that I ended up in burnout. Now that I have begun to receive the Father's love and see that the Father is drawing each of us individually to be His sons and daughters, I have found the missing link.

Some years ago I heard the Lord say, "First it will be individual sons, then the Bride will follow." It must be this way because the Bride will not be an orphaned Bride. The Bride will emerge fully cognisant of her status as the daughter of the Father and the Father will take her on His arm to the marriage of the Lamb. The Son will marry a Bride who is fully secure in sonship. As we rise into our sonship as individuals, the corporate Bride is going to come forth.

There is a direct correlation between coming into our true identity in sonship as *individuals* and the emergence of the Bride. The Bride of Christ, like the Body of Christ, is a *corporate* entity. The Bride can have no vestige of orphanness in her, therefore as individual identity in sonship matures, it naturally follows that the outcome will be the multi-faceted Bride of Christ, His Body. We can see this embryonically in communities of sons and daughters around the world, individuals synthesising to display a unified body; a foretaste of what is to come. I am beginning to fall in love again with the Body of Christ and see, even in places where there has been disillusionment, how much God loves people and is calling them into spiritual family and community.

I have no interest in promoting 'my ministry.' My major interest is to promote *your* ministry, to release who *you* are meant to be. We are not all meant to be bible teachers or 'worship leaders.' God is bringing forth the manifold wisdom that will be seen by the principalities and powers. (Ephesians 3:10) The many folds (manifold) of wisdom come through every individual. There is a particular aspect of the wisdom of God that comes through me. Equally, a different aspect of God's wisdom comes through who you are. It doesn't matter whether you perceive yourself to be in 'ministry' or not. You could be a car mechanic but if Christ is overflowing from you, *you are in ministry*. The personality of Jesus oozing from you creates ministry automatically. Part of my prophetic mandate is to open people's eyes to see this reality.

The corporate inheritance is conditional on the individual inheritance. I can see the connection. That is why I want to impart and equip so that others may emerge. I want to work myself out of a job, so to speak, so that the whole Body of Christ will enter her inheritance.

CHAPTER NINE

The Fulfilment
Of Prophecy

When we enter into our inheritance we are entering into the fulfilment of prophecy. True prophecy is meant to be fulfilled!

I believe in personal prophecy. I have been given and have spoken some very significant prophetic words myself.

In my opinion, however, personal prophecy has become too common. As a result it has become devalued and has lost credibility. We are overloaded with prophetic words. Many people are carrying prophetic promises and personal prophetic words that have been spoken over them. Some have carried these for twenty, thirty, forty years and more without seeing them fulfilled.

I am not interested any longer in just giving another prophetic word. What really interests me is seeing people come into the *fulfilment* of prophecy.

Many people are frustrated and even depressed because they don't see those prophetic words being fulfilled. One of the reasons for this frustration is that we misunderstand how prophetic words are actually fulfilled.

Generally speaking, we have received prophetic words when we are in a state of orphanness, slavery and fear. We then carry these prophecies for years, round and round in the wilderness, but we never enter into the actual fulfilment of them. I had some very significant prophecies myself, from some very prominent ministries. I wrote them in journals, but I still ended up in problems in my spiritual journey. Here is my observation of why we don't see the prophetic fulfilled:

Almost without exception, the fulfilment of the prophetic word looks *different* to the spoken prophetic word.

Let me clarify this. We receive a word of prophecy and we are encouraged. Maybe we write it down in a journal and hope it will someday come true. Oftentimes we get frustrated because it never seems to be fulfilled.

I received a word once from one of the foremost prophetic ministers in the world. One line was, "Stephen, you will be an anchor point for churches around the world." When I received it, I immediately thought, "Big international ministry!" I was ordering my private jet (not likely) and getting measured for my white suit! That prophetic word is currently being fulfilled but it looks *nothing like* I thought it would. We can miss the fulfilment of prophetic words if we expect it to look exactly like the word spoken.

What I am saying is very biblical. Throughout Scripture, the fulfilment of the prophetic word often looked very different from what the spoken prophecy described. Take, for example, the Day of Pentecost. The Holy Spirit descended upon the waiting disciples and they came from the Upper Room out to the street—*and they were perceived as being drunk.*

I remember, during the 1990s, when the church I was part of, in Belfast, was hit by a powerful move of the Spirit. Many people, including myself, were heavily intoxicated in the Spirit. On one occasion, a police patrol car turned up at the front of the church and two police officers got out. They were investigating a complaint of mass drunkenness in the street outside the church building. I was one of the people who attempted to explain to the policemen that these people "…are not drunk as you suppose…" (Acts 2:15) but were under the influence of Holy Spirit. The police were sceptical but eventually got into their patrol car and left.

This was how it appeared on the Day of Pentecost, drunks spilling out of the 'Upper Room' pub into the street. Some onlookers accused them of being "filled with new wine." (Acts 2:13) Then Peter stood up and spoke, "…THIS IS THAT…" This undignified inebriation, this drunkenness, was *that* which was prophesied by the prophet Joel.

This is how Joel's mighty army was described in the original prophetic word:

> *"A great and powerful people;*
> *their like has never been before,*
> *nor will be again after them*
> *through the years of all generations.*
>
> *Fire devours before them,*
> *and behind them a flame burns…*
> *Their appearance is like the appearance*
> *of horses,*
> *and like war horses they run.*
> *…they leap on the tops of the mountains,*
> *…Like warriors they charge, like soldiers they*
> *scale the wall.*
> *…They leap upon the city, they run upon the*
> *walls."*
> —JOEL 2:2-9

A powerful prophecy…but what did its fulfilment look like? It looked like some tipsy drunkards. But *THIS* is *THAT*.

Prophecy spoken…prophecy fulfilled.

Would you or I have had the spiritual know-how to make the same connection that Peter made, the connection between Joel's mighty army and the intoxicated disciples? Would we have recognised 'this' as being *that*? Do we have the discernment to recognise it *now*?

Another example, which many people missed, was the prophetic expectation about the coming Messiah. It had risen to such a level that Israel fully expected the Messiah to ride into Jerusalem, raise an army, and oust the Roman occupiers. Yes, there are prophecies about 'the suffering Servant' (Isaiah 53) but they seemed to have been overshadowed by ideas of a warrior-king even greater than David. That was the expectation but what did the fulfilment look like? It looked like a tiny baby in a manger. A baby in all respects like any other human baby.

Israel did not recognise Him because they were locked into an expectation that the Messiah must be *this*. Not *that* tiny baby, crying, kicking, soiling the swaddling clothes. But *this* is *that* which was prophesied by the prophets. Only a few shepherds and some Eastern *astrologers* recognised the coming of God on earth.

We have great difficulty entering into promise because we do not recognise the baby in the manger. I don't mean that we don't recognise *Jesus*; I mean that we do not recognise God's manifestation in what is small, weak and seemingly ordinary. Promise, fulfilment and inheritance invariably comes differently to our expectations of how it *should* come.

The Church has largely missed the fulfilment of the prophetic expectation of the 1980s and 1990s. Revival was prophesied and eagerly expected, and many were disappointed when it apparently didn't come. My belief is that something *did* appear, as a 'baby,' in absolute weakness. Many missed it but it is growing up now, hidden from the mainstream Church and from the world, but the time will come when it will be seen. Our eyes need to be opened to see what God is *actually* doing.

You may think your destiny cannot be anything other than having a high profile and you may feel frustrated because that is not happening. Let me assure you that God knows what He is doing. God is not that interested in putting His sons and daughters on platforms and stages. The Church needs to get down off the stage! My sense is that God's plan for the Church is to reorientate not only our belief and our experience, but *how* we actually *outwork* it.

If you are weary of looking into the elusive future, wondering when that prophetic word is ever going to come to pass, take another look in a different direction. Seek to be led to a baby in a stable, somewhere behind the main thoroughfare. Maybe destiny in your life is manifesting itself in weakness, in vulnerability, and in smallness. This is how it begins, *then* it grows into prophetic fulfilment.

CHAPTER TEN

Moses-Style Leadership Is Giving Way To Joshua-Style Leadership

Joshua's style of leadership was very different from Moses' style of leadership. What is coming forth in the Body of Christ is a Joshua style of leadership.

'Joshua' leadership does not, at first, seem as powerful and dynamic as 'Moses' leadership. It *appears* to have less anointing, because it is not required to demonstrate spectacular signs and wonders *by itself*, but it has an anointing to release *the Body of Christ* to do it. The late John Wimber personified this. He was more interested in 'equipping the saints' to do the works of the Kingdom than having the limelight on himself. He would often slip away from conferences early, leaving his young apprentices to 'do the stuff.' Jesus gave John Wimber a mandate to the Body of Christ. It was, plainly and simply, "I want My Church back!" Let me say as strongly as I can, that has not changed! The Lord still wants His Church back! He wants the *whole* Body to be equipped for ministry.

A Joshua leadership is not obviously charismatic; it does not eclipse everyone else. Joshua leadership *equips* and *releases* everyone else. We will find, as we read through the first few chapters of Joshua, that Joshua did not go ahead of the people and smite the Jordan with a rod of authority. Rather, he sent the people *ahead* of *him*, led by the priests carrying the Ark of the Covenant. It seems to suggest that Joshua stood aside to ensure that the others passed over first.

The Body of Christ has not come into the maturity that God wants it to come into. There are different reasons for this, but one that I wish to highlight is that ministers and leaders have not sufficiently equipped *the saints* for the work of ministry. I suspect that Joshua was not as individually charismatic as Moses, but that is because he had a different leadership function. Dare I suggest that a 'big ministry' that works in the conference setting is *less* effective in equipping everyone to step into their promise, in contrast to a ministry which does not draw the focus onto itself but shines the spotlight on the members of the Body.

This different style of leadership that God is raising up is for the purpose of calling the Body of Christ to move forward into promise. This leadership has a different mandate and a different gift-cluster, a different type of anointing. In a very inadequate way, I believe that I have the heart of a Joshua. I am not called to the big conference event or to a high profile ministry. What I want, however, is to push *you* ahead of me into *your* destiny.

As long as we place all our hope in an anointed leader on a platform, we will not be equipped to enter into *our* destiny. For the Body of Christ to increase, the gap between leaders and the people must decrease (John 3:30). It is no longer a matter of certain individuals being anointed; it is a matter of the Body of Christ being anointed.

You may not be anointed to have thousands gather to you, but you have an equal capacity for anointing as those that do gather the crowds.

I know a man who is not obviously not called to traditional ministry. But he is highly anointed in other 'unexpected' areas. He is very anointed with his hands in craftsmanship, as well as in mechanics and in fixing things. I once witnessed him working at a problem in a car engine. He was leaning a lot on his intuition. It dawned on me that he was actually flowing in words of knowledge and words of wisdom to fix a mechanical problem in a car engine. His 'magic touch' is nothing less than the anointing of the Spirit.

We are all meant to have a foundational revelation of our belovedness, our chosenness, that we are in Christ, justified, indwelled by the Spirit, etcetera etcetera. Beyond that basic revelation, further revelation will flow to what our individual calling is. If you are not called to teach the Bible, the Bible will not be opened up to you in the same way that it is opened to those who are meant to teach the

Body of Christ. *But* anointing and revelation *will* flow to you in the area that you are called to, whether or not it fits within your current definition of 'ministry.' We need to understand that there is no such thing as the sacred-secular divide. *All* areas to which we are called are manifestations of the risen Christ.

This is how I believe the multi-faceted wisdom of God is going to be revealed through the Church to principalities and powers. (Ephesians 3:10) The whole creation is waiting for manifestation of the sons of God (Romans 8:19), but this manifestation is not going to come primarily through seminars and conferences. They are but a tiny part of it. Creation's longing will be satisfied when the sons of God become increasingly revealed in their unique individuality and calling, and the symbiosis of this in a Body, the Church.

God is calling the Church to maturity, through revealing Himself as Father to every individual. The Bride cannot emerge until every member is living in the Father's love.

Getting a revelation of the multi-varied gifting of every person, and a revelation of the wholeness of the Church, removes a lot of pressure from us as individuals. You, as an individual, are not supposed to reach the world. You are part of *a corporate body* whose commission it is to reveal the love of God. As you receive love you will, increasingly, manifest who God is *in you*. You will be free of feeling the pressure to be someone else. And you will celebrate the fact that God is manifesting Himself through you in a different way than through others.

I am not looking for a 'superstar' type of leadership any more. The time of the superstars is over. The 'nameless-faceless' generation (prophesied in the 80s and 90s) is now here. What is more, *leadership* is intended to be 'nameless' and 'faceless.' That is what God is looking for. God is looking for Joshua-style leadership to catalyse the entry of the Church into promise and inheritance. Maybe you are one of those leaders.

CHAPTER ELEVEN

Be Strong And Courageous!

The exhortation to be strong and courageous is repeated again and again in the first chapter of Joshua. Why is this rubbed into Joshua so that he really gets it?

Strength and courage is required to enter the Promised Land to an extent that it is not required to come out of Egypt. When we come out of Egypt, our faith is in our Saviour. We place our faith away from ourselves to Him. We also place our faith in those who are leaders to us.

When it comes to entering Promise and Inheritance, however, we need to focus our faith back to ourselves. Not on ourselves exactly, but on Christ *within* us. This takes a different revelation than the revelation of Christ rescuing us from slavery.

Strength and courage is needed to possess the land. Why? Because, when we look at ourselves, we know full well that we cannot do it by ourselves. We are weak and inadequate, we have a 'dark side,' we have no illusions about ourselves. In spite of all this, we need to have the courage that comes with the revelation that Christ is within us and His power is working through our weakness.

I needed to come to terms with being 'Stephen Hill.' Through a wilderness process and the dealings of God my spiritual grandiosity was burst like a bubble. I needed to face myself with my strengths, my weaknesses, my sense of being called, my vulnerability to temptation. I needed to reconcile myself to the reality that God is pleased to live within me.

Part of my inheritance is to write. It is not easy to put oneself out there for people to either love, hate or (worst of all) to ignore. But, if we are to enter into our inheritance, we have to accept our own voice and our own style. We need to find our unique expression and live with it, because God will not anoint anything else.

When God says, "Be strong and courageous," it is not to give us 'strength' and 'courage' as such. Strength and courage are not substances in themselves. They come when perfect love drives out fear (1 John 4:18). Believe me, love and compassion will take you to places that you would not go otherwise.

I have an interest in military history. In reading about it, I discovered that the majority of the soldiers who received medals for valour in war did not do that great deed because they had some mysterious substance of 'bravery' within them. They didn't even do these brave deeds for the great cause of their country. When it was analysed, they mostly acted out of concern for their fellow-soldiers beside them. It was a sense of camaraderie and compassion that motivated them, born from the brotherhood of soldiers on the battle-field. The essence of courage is actually *love.*

Love will automatically impart strength and courage into us. Compassionate love will take us where we need to go. It will propel us beyond our fears, beyond our assumptions, and beyond our prejudices.

When I was a teenager I was play-fighting with my older brother. He kneed me very forcefully in the groin. Later, as I was urinating, I was shocked to see spots of bright red blood on the white porcelain toilet bowl. Fearful of some internal haemorrhage, I ran downstairs to tell my dad who was sitting in his chair reading the newspaper.

Without hesitation, my dad prayed for my healing. His prayer was instinctive because, if he hesitated to think about, he doesn't actually believe in the gift of healing. He holds a 'dispensationalist' view that the gifts of the Spirit are not for today. But his compassion for me, his son, kicked in and he used his fatherly authority, and I was healed. He still didn't change his theology. Love took him to a place in faith that he would never otherwise have gone to.

When God speaks, the substance of the word that He speaks is deposited inside us and made real in us. God does not speak and then leave us to our own devices to fulfil

His word. God's Word is synonymous with His life-giving Spirit.

The reason why we need be strong and courageous is because entry into our promised inheritance requires something in us that exodus doesn't. It was primarily Moses who needed strength and courage to lead the people out of Egypt because God made him a talismanic leader. But without that style of leader, we need to find the strength and courage *within ourselves.*

I look into the future and I see that God is bringing forth the Body of Christ. God is raising up the *whole Body*, *every person*, into authority.

I never assume that I am more spiritually mature than the people I may be speaking to. One of the big deceptions is that those of us up the front, with titles, behind podiums, with microphones, are closer to God than those of us sitting in the 'congregation.' That is not how God sees it. The rug is being pulled out from all forms of 'apartheid' in the Church—clergy/lay, sacred/secular, staff/student, stage/floor, ministry team/congregation. These are manmade categorisations. You may not be gifted in the same area but you have *equal potential* for maturity of heart. Some of the most spiritual in the kingdom of God are unknown, they have no public profile.

Have you ever heard of Watchman Nee? Yes, I assume you have. He is well known and many people will recognise the name. But, tell me this: Have you ever heard of Margaret Barber? Do you know who *she* is?

Very few people have heard of this obscure woman. She was a little English lady, who was the spiritual parent of Watchman Nee. All that he became was down to her influence in his life. Watchman Nee commented that Miss Barber was, by far, the most spiritual (closest to the Lord) person he had ever met. She never left the little village in China where she lived for many years, and died in obscurity. Her gravestone was smashed to pieces during the Cultural Revolution, so no one even knows the location of her grave. But her spirit spawned a massive move of God which still continues today.

Strength and courage is required because you cannot enter into your destiny on the back of the faith of others. Yes, you can receive the mantle of those fathers and mothers in the Lord who have gone before, but you *yourself* will need to have the faith to step into and walk in what *you* have received. You need to believe in who God is, but, maybe more importantly, you need to believe in who God is specifically within *you*. Only a supernatural impartation of courage will fortify you enough to cross every obstacle between you and your promised inheritance.

CHAPTER TWELVE

Returning To The Future

"Then you shall return to the land of your possession and possess it." — JOSHUA 1:15

Entering into inheritance and promise is a *return* to something that has always been there. As I said before, the blueprint of our destiny is already hardwired into our humanity. It is a wonderful paradox that moving forward into the new also feels like a deep homecoming. When you get a sense of your destiny it resonates deeply with the ancient pulsations of your heart.

I have observed something in my own life and in the lives of others who come into the love of the Father. The Spirit leads us *back* to familiar places. The Spirit leads us to *return*.

Orphanness makes us run away from home, but we, like the prodigal son (Luke 15) are led back home to receive the Father's favour in the place where we departed from it. We may eventually be sent out again but *returning* is part of entering into promise.

I suspect that many of you are given a heart desire to go back to where you came from. Either that happens or circumstances leave you no option. Do not be dismayed at this. This return is a pathway towards your inheritance.

Why is a forward movement into destiny also a return? That sounds like a contradiction.

As our false identity and false motivation recedes we become much more authentic. As a result of this, elements of who we *really* are re-emerge and come back to us. We could say that we *return* to the person God has created us to be. We also return to things, attributes and interests, that God has put into us from childhood.

Some years ago the Lord spoke to me. This is what He said:

"What you have surrendered in lordship is given back to you in sonship."

That took me aback; in fact, it stunned me. But it is, for the most part, true.

When we come to Christ we submit to Him as Lord of our lives. We lay *everything* down at His feet. Lordship requires this. Many things that were idols to us have to be surrendered to the lordship of Christ.

But then something happens—something that I did not have an inkling of until I came into the experience of sonship. God offered my desires and interests *back* to me.

He said, "You can have them back now. They are not an idol anymore. In fact they can be used for My glory."

In sonship God wants to give our humanity back to us, our unique identity back to us, our interests and passions back to us. He does so because He is confident that our heart now belongs to Him and we can be trusted because we have the hearts of sons and daughters. You see, love has fulfilled the Law. You cannot legislate for those who are walking in love (Galatians 5:23). Paul the apostle also said, "To the pure all things are pure, but to the defiled and unbelieving nothing is pure." (Titus 1:15) Purity is an issue of what is in your heart. In sonship you get your initiative back. Our human personality is given back to us as an instrument for God inside us to express Himself through.

For example, I have returned to reading some of the books that I gave up reading because of a misplaced zeal for the Kingdom. These are not sinful things; they are innocent things that I cast off because I thought they weighed me down in running the race. I have a renewed interest in nature, in history, in books, in art, in films, cars, motor-bikes and more. I had laid all these things down on the altar of consecrating myself to God, and I don't doubt that it was important at the time but they have come back to me.

Many people, including myself, who go through transition and receive an experience of the love of the Father, do not immediately go into new and unexplored territories.

More than often, they *return* to the familiar, to what they once knew. Maybe they go back to their home town, their old employment, back to what they were trying to run away from. Instead of running from the simple, even mundane, things of life, they find a joy in returning to them. This is not a backward step; it is a step *forward,* because entering into future promise and inheritance *involves a return.*

If the blueprint of our destiny is already hardwired into our human personality, we need to return to that humanity. Religion has driven a wedge between the 'spiritual,' 'godly' things, and that which is 'earthy' and 'human.' Some aspects of 'new mysticism' and 'extreme prophetic' have divided what is 'spiritual' from the baseness of the human condition but, unknown to them, they are being more influenced by Greek philosophy than a biblical worldview. The supernatural life of Christianity is intended to take place at the level of human reality, not escape from it.

If you are surprised to find yourself going back to your roots, maybe moving home again, returning to your old employment, don't see it as a regression; see it as a *progression.* A deep work is being done in your heart. I had to go back to Belfast after a life-changing time in New Zealand. I restored my relationship with my parents. I had carried some very significant prophecies and I thought I would be catapulted into an awesome ministry, but I *returned* to my home city so that I could restore my heart of sonship to my parents. I needed to return to the place where I had lived with fig leaves, to learn to live *without* any fig leaves. I had lived a shame-based life there, running from who I really was. To move forward, I had to go *back*.

When I was in my twenties and thirties, my heart was closed to my parents. I believed that they were a hindrance to me moving in the things of God. I wanted to abandon my parents to the care of my sisters, but I had to *return*. Out of the heart of being a son to them, I returned to love my parents again, to have compassion for them, to serve them.

As He entered His ministry, Jesus, "...*returned* in the power of the Spirit to Galilee..." (Luke 4:14). Then He came "to Nazareth, where He had been brought up." (Luke 4:16) In His local synagogue He was given the pulpit to preach a sermon. He took up the scroll of Isaiah and began to read (Isaiah 61:1,2, Luke 4:16-21):

> *"The Spirit of the Lord is upon me,*
> *because he has anointed me..."*

After reading the passage, He proclaimed:

> *"Today, this Scripture has been fulfilled in*
> *your hearing."*

Jesus *returned* in the power of the Spirit to His hometown and his local synagogue; it was a necessary prerequisite to going into public ministry. If the same happens to you, it is so that *you*, the "carpenter's son, born out of wedlock" will re-assert an identity as one upon whom the Spirit of the Lord is.

When we come into the Father's love we are not being propelled into some fantasy world of amazing experiences, like a 'Walter Mitty' Christianity. Our inheritance is inextricably linked with a *return* to our most authentic selves.

> *"You shall return to the land of your possession*
> *and possess it."*

I have written some books, which I am very proud of. They may not be bestsellers but they are an authentic expression of *me*. Writing these books was a return to who I really am. When I was a child I showed real promise at creative writing. Due to my extreme legalistic upbringing this was suppressed and for many years I did not operate according to my true bent. Then, many years later, when Love came to me, my interest and ability in writing began to re-emerge. You see, it is within my destiny to be a writer and it is simultaneously a return to my childhood abilities and interests.

The Bible says, "Train up a child in the way he should go; even when he is old he will not depart from it." (Proverbs 22:6) The Hebrew understanding of this is not about teaching your child how to behave or use good manners. It is, actually, about understanding how God has created them, what are their unique interests and strengths, and shaping them according to these.

Religion has deceived us that becoming like Jesus means a departure from who we really are. Nothing could be farther from the truth. The 'death of self' is actually the death of a falsely constructed identity. God wants to reduce us down to become naked, free and clothed with the covering of His love.

God can lead us to return to our original place of belonging (even if it was a negative experience) so that it can be redeemed. When I forgave my parents from the heart, and when I repented from my heart of how I had treated them, I began to hear my father saying things that I had longed for many years to hear him say. Things like, "I'm proud of you, son," or "You're a fine man, Stephen!" I no longer needed this affirmation from my earthly father, since my heavenly Father was affirming me, but my return to Belfast returned that which had been missing between me and my dad.

God-reality is not some sort of ethereal mysticism. True spirituality is a connection between heaven and earth, between the transcendent and the immanent, between spirit and material. The physical realm *is* spiritual. Our eyes need to be opened to see the interface of the divine and the human, the eternal order and the created order. Immanuel is 'God with us.'

Your destiny will look somehow familiar to you. It may be beyond your imagination but it will also run along ancient tracks and familiar lines. You heart will recognise it because it is already deeply planted within you.

CHAPTER THIRTEEN

The Inheritance Is A Place Of Rest

"The Lord your God is providing you with a place of rest and will give you this land."
— JOSHUA 1:13

To come into promise and inheritance is to come into a place of *rest*. It is to be healed of insecurity and then to be free of striving. God has promised us a place of rest. Rest is a rare commodity in today's society and, sadly, in today's Christianity. Very few churches promote a culture of rest. But rest is our inheritance and God longs to bring us into His rest.

Hebrews 4:11 exhorts us to "strive to enter rest." I had a problem with the word 'strive.' Surely striving to rest is a contradiction in terms. Then I realised that entering into rest was the biggest battle my soul was facing. Why 'strive' to enter rest? Because the enemy of your soul is continually trying to engage you in combat by your own strength. But that is not how the victory is won. When you are under attack you win by lying down and resting. You conquer by resting in the fact that Jesus has already defeated Satan.

God has promised to prepare a table for us in the presence of our enemies (Psalm 23: 5)

Graham Cooke tells a story of a vision (or a dream) he had. He was standing on a battlefield and a huge army of demons was about to attack him. Then the Lord appeared dressed as a very high class waiter, with a black long tailed suit, white bow tie, napkin draped over his arm. Graham was dumbfounded. He was incredulous when the Lord said, "Will you be starting with the melon or the soup, today, sir?" Graham was thinking: *Here I am on a battlefield about to fight for my very life against the hordes of hell and You, Lord, are playing some joke about melon or soup!* Then it dawned on him. The Lord was setting a table for him in the presence of his enemies!

When we come into rest, anointing and revelation have a free flow. To receive revelation you need to be able to relax in mystery, that is to say, you rest in what you *don't know*. It is very difficult for us to accept that it is not possible to know everything or to be able to master all the reasons why. We need to rest suspended in mystery, as if we are floating in a swimming pool.

As we come into sonship we are becoming more free to live without fig leaves and, as a result, to be honest with God, ourselves and others. God is not interested in our fig leaves, in who we *project* ourselves to be. Coming into rest is coming into the joyful acceptance of who we are. It may begin with resigning yourself out of exhaustion but then you will come to joyfully love yourself *with* your flaws, your idiosyncrasies, your quirkiness. Not everyone is even going to like or admire you but that's okay.

Sometimes we are looking for emotional healing because, deep down, we reject who we are. That is getting the cart before the horse. Coming to a place of acceptance of who we are will be a salve for emotional pain and wounding. I do not think we should be overly focused on inner healing as a goal. Allow divine love to come, bringing with it unconditional acceptance and the ability to heal whatever it needs to heal.

The truth is, we are just clay pots but we contain an eternal and priceless treasure. Paul was fully aware of this:

"For we have this treasure in earthen vessels that the all-surpassing power might be from God and not from us."
— 2 Corinthians 4:7

The earthen vessel is the acceptance of oneself without shame. Shame causes us to project a falsely constructed self as a fig leaf, but when love comes it loves you as you are, broken, weak and failing. Divine love even loves you when it sees the dark side of who you are. The dark side is the part of you that has not known love. When the light of love comes the hidden things of shame shrouded in darkness are exposed to love-light.

Love covers a multitude of sins in your heart. True transformation comes when the fig leaves are removed. A covering of glory is bestowed by the Father's favour allowing you to be naked and without shame. Nakedness is the Father's purpose for us. Adam and Eve were naked and unashamed before God. Why? Because they existed in the presence of pure love. Because they had not yet partaken of the knowledge of good and evil.

The knowledge of good and evil brings shame because it imposes a system of assessment based upon a distortion of the true character of God. The true character of God is a love that can be implicitly trusted to bring about our maximum good. Satan distorts this and snares us to make a judgment that God our loving Father is not who He says He is.

God does want to change us, there is no doubt about that. But He does so from a place of loving us without conditions. We are changed by the transformational power of His changeless love. He changes us away from our false selves into our true selves, designed by Him to authentically display Christ. Don't seek healing in order to be a clone of your hero (Christian or otherwise). Don't look to get emotionally healed into some sort of shiny, happy-go-lucky, plastic, 'no problems' Christian. Allow God to bring you to the acceptance of who you are, and to rest in that. Then you will discover that your promise begins to be attracted to you and you will move towards your inheritance.

When we come to a place of rest it is a homecoming to ourselves. **When you come fully home to yourself and God is fully at home within you, then you can receive God's gift.** The only way that you can really become at home to yourself is to allow God to fully inhabit your heart and to come fully into your identity and sonship. While you are under condemnation and while you are still trying to impress you can never come to a place of rest. This is why it is very important for us to become true to ourselves.

Some years ago, I went to Australia with a dear friend, a wonderful man. He has a winsome personality, and such a non-judgmental way with people that he is loved wherever he goes; he truly manifests the Father. He is also an extremely gifted communicator, with a hilarious sense of humour.

While we were in Canberra, we did a seminar in a local church. I was struggling. On the Sunday, my friend preached at the church and he and the congregation got on like a house on fire! When the service was over I was desperate to leave but I had to wait until the very end, because my friend was surrounded by people. He was in one corner with upwards of twenty people waiting to chat and hug him. I was standing in the opposite corner alone and feeling increasingly sorry for myself, with my orphanness hitting a peak.

I told him about this as we flew home. I told him how I

felt and how I began to compare myself to him. I considered seeing a counsellor for more inner healing. Then the Lord spoke clearly to me that, no matter how healed I became, I would *never* be like my friend. All the healing in the world can only ever make me be *me.*

Many people are wanting healing and wholeness but they are looking for it within the Tree of the Knowledge of Good and Evil. What do I mean by this? Well, we look at ourselves through the eyes of the knowledge of good and evil and, invariably, we see a huge need for improvement. The Tree of the Knowledge of Good and Evil will always measure us against a 'perfect' standard. We then seek healing to try and reach some idea of what 'perfection' may be. Little do we know that can *never* happen.

The only way to change is to allow love to enter in and it will bring healing with it; but you can also accept and even celebrate your brokenness. The knowledge of good and evil makes us compare ourselves to others; we want to be per-petually nice, shiny and happy. We seek healing to become something that religion or culture tells us is successful.

I am not trying to be anyone other than myself. I have come to accept, enjoy and be free to be Stephen Hill. I know that I am nothing special yet I am highly favoured. It is a paradox. I know my gifts, but I also know that others are more gifted in their areas. I am not constantly evalu-ating myself to try and iron out every quirk and idiosyncrasy in my personality. I trust God to change me by His love. I submit to my friends and those who know me who I welcome to speak into my life. But I have come to a place of rest—take me or leave me!

When we come home to ourselves, God can come home to us. The Trinity want to live and fully relax in us. The Godhead want to rest and fully express Themselves in us, individually and corporately.

Forgive me this language: When God is fully relaxed in us, then His personality can begin to blossom. God's personality on earth is suppressed because we, His desired incarnation, have not come home to ourselves. I think we would all agree that God's glory (the outpouring of His character and personality) has yet to be fully manifested on this earth and to the wider creation. Our Father, the Lord Jesus, and the Holy Spirit are not known enough!

We are all different facets of the diamond. We display aspects of God's character, but until we come home to ourselves in rest, our unique expressions of God will be stunted.

Entry into rest opens up our experiences of God's movements. God has entered rest and operates out of rest. It is only the true self that the Holy Spirit can overshadow and anoint. He cannot anoint a false self or a persona. When we come fully home to ourselves then God can come fully home within us. Relaxation makes way for incarnation. When the angel told Mary that she would be become pregnant with the Son of God, her response was, "Let it be to me according to your word." (Luke 1:38)

We have something of a revelation of Christ but of Him *external* to us. We now need a revelation of an *internal* Anointed One. A separated Christ in a high and distant heaven is not the hope of glory. It is Christ *within* us who is the hope of glory. (Colossians 1:27)

There needs to be a homecoming where the risen Christ intertwines with our personalities. Paul, in Colossians 1:27 refers to this as a 'mystery.' The biblical idea of mystery is not something enigmatic and confusing. It means that it was hidden until the time comes for it to be revealed. Paul's ministry was to unveil these hidden mysteries. These mysteries were part of God's plan but were hidden throughout the Old Testament period. One of the major mysteries, revealed by Paul is Christ *in us*, the hope of glory. I suspect this still remains a mystery to most of the Body of Christ. Christ, the fulness of the Godhead, within you, a human being! The sheer, brilliant *craziness* of this needs to come to us as a revelation!

Paul the apostle said, "By the grace of God I am what I am" (1 Corinthians 15:10). You come to a place of rest when you don't use fig leaves any more, you don't strive to improve yourself, but relax and say, "God, here I am. Take me as I am. I will not cover my nakedness any longer."

Coming to this point is very liberating. When you don't focus on yourself any longer you can really begin to live life and enjoy life and see others affected by your freedom.

One of the reasons why many Pentecostal/Charismatic Christians are not entering the inheritance is because they are wedded to a 'culture of excellence.' This culture separates those in ministry from those who are not, those who are highly competent from those who are not, those who are 'fashion forward' from those who are not. Or in the prophetic movement, the higher-level 'spiritual' is seen as more important than the lower-level 'secular.' These are all lies which need to be exposed if the Church is going to make progress in spiritual maturity.

Let me declare right now: *There is no sacred-secular divide.* You can rule and reign in Kingdom authority in your job as much *if not more* than if you weren't there. I once knew someone who was an engineering lecturer and his students so loved him that they asked him specifically to preach the Gospel to them on the last lecture of the term. Because the students initiated it he couldn't be disciplined for proselytising by the college authorities. This lecturer was a natural evangelist. Then he was employed on the staff of the church to sit in an office and come up with programmes for evangelism. His gifting was stymied. Why? Because there was a sacred-secular split operating. Perhaps he should have remained in his job where life and anointing flowed.

I heard a story recently about a young surgeon. The Lord told him that He was going to give him a healing ministry. What I like about this story is that the young man didn't quit being a surgeon. He didn't start healing crusades. He remained in his vocation as a medical doctor and the Lord used him to heal supernaturally as his hands touched his patients. As a surgeon he believed that supernatural power would flow through his hands. In the old paradigm, most likely, he would have renounced being a surgeon, but he has come to a place of rest in his vocation as a medical professional yet a conduit for supernatural healing power.

As we grow in our sonship, the issue of our lives is not so much to allow God in. He is already in our hearts. The real issue becomes; How do we allow God *out*? How can God express Himself through our lives? Any character issues that are being dealt with are to allow God to come more fully home in us, but also to allow He who is already inside us to manifest Himself more in our lives. Once the Body of Christ starts to recognise this, it will take a quantum leap forward. The Hope of Glory, Christ within us, will be seen by all.

Redemption Of Family Inheritance

The more you are established in your identity as a son or daughter of the Father, the more your family background begins to be redeemed. It may take a long time for this to be fully realised and for some it may not fully happen in this life, but we can have hope for it to *begin* happening.

I have seen a poster which says, "Forgiveness doesn't change the past, but it does enlarge the future." I do not agree. True forgiveness, *heart* forgiveness, *does* change the past, or, to be more exact, it changes *our perception* of the past. When we forgive from the heart and the heart is healed, the past no longer has any hold over us and it does not determine our present or future experience of life. In fact, the future cannot be enlarged unless the past is settled and brought to closure in our hearts.

In the light of love, the past looks different. Before my heart was healed, all I could see in my dad was passivity and inadequacy. Now he is a hero to me. I see his faithfulness, his bravery and his desire for his family to be secure.

There is redemption within the natural family lines. Some years ago, my uncle (Mum's brother) uncovered some old family photographs. One of the photographs especially impacted me. It was of my great-uncle (my mum's uncle) in First World War officers uniform. I researched into it a little; it turns out he was a captain of a cavalry regiment. My mum told me that he had a bullet hole in his thigh that he could put his fist into. He was wearing a row of medals, including a Military Cross awarded for "an act or acts of exemplary gallantry during active operations against the enemy on land to all members, of any rank in Our Armed Forces."

There is thread of valour and bravery in my family background. My mother saved the life of a drowning child. I have personally saved the life of two people (or at least prevented serious injury); one person whose clothing caught fire and I beat out the flames with my bare hand, the other was a profoundly deaf child I pulled back from being hit by a speeding car.

You will find that the inheritance in your family line is redeemable and available to you. When God begins to redeem us and restore the heart of sonship to us, it will include the redemption of many things that we are not even aware of. God is showing me parts of myself that I wasn't even aware of as a child but when my heart is opened up I can begin to walk in them.

When I was a child I had a gift for words and for writing. I had success very early when my stories were published in school magazines. I also had some of my writing published in a school textbook. Then, when I was about 7 years old, I was shamed in the area of my gifting and I shut it down for many years. I left school at 16, worked faithfully for many years but was often frustrated.

In 1999, I did a university degree, while working at the same time for an investment company. It was an itch that needed to be scratched. To my surprise I rediscovered my gift for academic success, graduating with a First-Class Honours degree on top of my university year! It was only when I got the heart of a son back that I was able to uncover my created identity and find success out of it. Success will come to what God has created you for. God has created us for success, not based on 'celebrity' standards, but joy and pleasure in work that flows from your truest identity.

Some years ago, I was in Australia and the Lord spoke to me and told me that He would give me the inheritance of my father, Jack Hill. God said, "Stephen, you will receive that which you did not work for and you will enter into what your earthly father couldn't enter into."

My dad is 85 and he never really did what he wanted to do in life. My dad never came into who he fully was; he never fulfilled his potential. He wanted to join the police but he couldn't do that. Fear and religion have robbed him of many things. He will never fulfil his true potential in this life. The Lord said to me, "Your dad's heart desires are held by Me in a heavenly storehouse and they are available for whoever wants them. He will not lose it. In some way he will enter into it. The inheritance of the past is not lost." I do not know the full ramifications of what that means but I receive it in my heart.

Orphan-spirited Christianity does not have any understanding of blessing flowing through generations. Orphan-spirited Christianity is more taken up with curses than blessings. It is focused on how to be free of the negative but doesn't fully see the positive. The Bible is overwhelmingly more positive than negative. Take, for example, Deuteronomy 5: 9,10:

> *"…for I the LORD your GOD am a jealous God, visiting the iniquity of the fathers on the children to the third and fourth generation of those that hate me, but showing steadfast love to the thousandth generation of those who love me and keep my commandments."*

In other words, the consequences of family judgment and curse are only meted out to three and four generations but blessing flows to *a thousand generations*. When we forgive from the heart the curse is removed and we can access the blessing of a thousand generations. The consequences of negative behaviour are supposed to only last for three or four generations but unless you forgive from the heart and restore the heart of being a son or daughter, the residual curse still hounds you. Negative stuff is more about our orphanness than a specific family curse. Coming out of orphan-hearted identity will *automatically* make most curses null and void. Then the blessing of a thousand generations is released to flow.

This is why heart forgiveness and having a heart of sonship is so important because it changes our perspective to see blessing instead of curse, to realise the positive instead of the negative. In the Tree of Knowledge my own dad was legalistic and passive, and did not father me as he should have done. But in the light of love, I see all his *positive* characteristics. He is my hero, because love sees him as he really is. I see blessing flowing now instead of curse.

When I was about to become a father for the first time, I asked my dad to bless me. He was shocked but I could see that he was pleased. He and Mum sat beside me, one on each side and prayed a prayer over me. Something shifted; I felt equipped in a way I had never done. My parents' prayer, albeit couched in religious language, tied up many loose ends for me. God honoured it because He knows the importance of blessing flowing through generations.

I have a friend who did not have a good relationship with his father. He went to visit his father who was in his nineties and in the advanced stages of Alzheimers. The night before my friend left to catch a flight home, he was going to bed and it suddenly occurred to him to ask his dad for a blessing. His dad had gone to bed and my friend had to catch an early flight the next morning.

The next morning my friend got up, had a bite of breakfast and was ready to take a taxi to the airport. He looked towards his dad's bedroom door but it was closed and he was tempted to leave the old man sleeping. Then it occurred to him that this may be the last time he would see his dad alive so he mustered his courage and went into the bedroom, where he found his dad sitting up in bed. He blurted out his request for a blessing. Amazingly his dad's face lit up, confusion cleared away and focus came to his eyes. For a few minutes the old man was totally unaffected by the Alzheimers and he agreed to give his blessing. It only took seconds and my friend had to rush to the airport. His father died not long afterwards. But my friend said that this experience of being blessed by his father resolved issues that he had been carrying for many years. When love comes, restoration comes and what is stolen begins to be recompensed.

Your natural children are your inheritance. The Jews understand this, but Christians have largely lost this understanding. In the past there were missionaries who left their kids at home and went off to the mission field. The wellbeing of the children was sacrificed for the sake of the mission. That practice is thankfully outdated but it was not of God. God is very interested, invested in and connected to generational blessings. I find it fascinating to see family likeness across generations. My niece was born long after my grandmother died but she is the spitting image of her. I saw some photographs of my ancestors recently, from the time of World War 1. The young men (my great-uncles who I never met) have some of the exact same features that I have.

HEART FORGIVENESS OF PAST GENERATIONS

Recently I was in a meeting and the speaker led us all again in the prayer for heart forgiveness. I thought I had done that already, but the Holy Spirit led me in a way that surprised me. He led me to forgive *my grandfather*.

This brought a fresh insight to me. Forgiving generations previous to our parents is not so much an issue of coming into a relationship of sonship to the Father. Rather, it is an issue of *expanding* our sonship to *redeem our inheritance*.

This is an important point so let me explain it. In order to come into a sonship connection with the Father, we need to forgive our parents from the heart. That is the doorway which reactivates our connection to our heavenly Father.

But if the Lord leads us to heart-forgive other people such as grandparents, and other authority figures, it has ramifications, not so much for restoring the heart of sonship, but for restoring the *authority* of sonship.

For example, your teacher may have called you dumb (stupid). That will affect you to the degree that you are already insecure. My brother's son was bullied at school, but it didn't affect him as much as it could have done because he was very secure in the fact that his parents loved him and knew who he really was. My nephew was confident in his uniqueness because it was instilled in him by his parents, so the jibes of other kids didn't bother him to the extent that they could have done if he had had a foundation of being unloved.

So when I was invited to revisit heart forgiveness again, my initial thought was, "What do we need to do this again for?" But, as I stood there, it was not my parents who were impressed upon my heart. No, the Lord brought someone else to my inner sight; it was my *grandfather*. My grandfather had lived a successful life. He was a top executive in one of the most successful companies in the world, chauffeur driven to work every day. He owned a number of properties. He was very influential at many levels. But, in 1970, there was a schism in the Exclusive Brethren and my grandparents never spoke to us again!

It dawned on me that my grandfather's influence (for the good) was stolen from me. He was always immaculately dressed in a pin-striped three-piece suit, complete with gold pocket watch and Homburg hat. I like to dress well. I like to wear well-cut clothes. I actually enjoy wearing suits. I used to be under bondage to wear a suit to church, but now

I'm under bondage not to wear a suit to church! I jest but I am making a serious point too.

In my life, I have struggled with low self-confidence. I lived many years not fulfilling my true potential. I had jobs that were below my capability and which were not well paid. But my grandfather did not have a low self-esteem. He confidently carried success and responsibility. His influence in my life was stolen away from me.

After praying that prayer of forgiveness about my grandfather something has shifted for me. I don't fully know what it is. I guess it is the opening of an ancient well. All I can say for sure is that there was a part of me that had never confidently flourished in who I was, but when I forgave my grandfather from the heart, a golden seam of inheritance was unlocked. His influence, which had been stolen from me, began to work again in my soul. A sense of success came back to the core of my being.

If the Spirit leads you in these areas of forgiving people (after you have already forgiven your parents) from the heart, it is to restore more of what was stolen from you. It is about *expanding* your sonship identity. The inheritance that is available opens up more and more.

The inheritance can be redeemed in the past and in the future. My childhood was repressed because of fears in our family. My father's brother died in childhood from a head injury received when he fell from a low wall he was climbing. As a result of this family history we were never allowed to climb trees when we were children, especially when my grandparents were present. A few years back I was walking past a large tree and I heard the Father prompting me to climb it. I climbed it and something was redeemed. It gave me more confidence to be a husband and a father myself. I am very grateful that my kids have a grandfather on Becky's side who is helping them to learn how to swim and dive so they are not hampered by the fears that I was hampered with.

This doesn't only work in the natural realm; it works in the spiritual realm as well. We carry spiritual DNA from the past. Anointing is meant to grow exponentially with each generation. The mantle that was on great men and women of the past is meant to double for those who come after them. Why has this not happened? Could it be because we have not have hearts of sons towards them? In our orphan-heartedness we have not recognised spiritual fathers and mothers. Watchman Nee had a son's heart for Margaret Barber. Has anyone received a double portion of what Smith Wigglesworth had?

Everything that God has ever given to our spiritual forebears is available to us. It is sitting in heavenly store-houses awaiting our use. Can we, by faith, avail ourselves of it? Sons and daughters can have it, if they ask for it. The Holy Spirit is the custodian of the treasure store.

The revelation and anointing that our forebears carried did not die with them. That revelation is available for us now. It may have already come out or it may still be coming. It is not locked up to us and rendered unavailable. It is available for us, sitting out there in the realm of Spirit. It is available as we begin to have hearts of sons and daughters towards those in the past.

According to 2 Kings 13:20,21, Elisha's bones had residual potency in them. They had resurrection life so that when a dead man was thrown into the pit where the bones were buried, there was enough resurrection life in the bones to restore life to that man. Amazing!

Heart forgiveness of those who have gone before actually opens the inheritance that is available. As far as God is concerned, the mysteries of the past are not locked up, they are not stolen, we have not lost them. Just as the mantle of Elijah dropped from him and was caught by Elisha, their riches are available to us.

Entering By The Sole Of The Foot

Joshua chapter 1 verse 3 says:

"Every place that the sole of your foot will tread upon, I have given to you just as I promised to Moses."

This is crucial. It is one of the major reasons why we are not able to enter into our promised destiny. It is a particular problem for Pentecostals and Charismatics and people influenced by the prophetic movement. Remember my earlier point about entry being different to exodus. Exodus happens by an outstretched arm and a spectacular miracle. But promise and the inheritance is entered into by the sole of the foot.

If you look at the sole of your foot it is very small in area compared with a land to possess. Promise and inheritance is entered into by the sole of the foot. Where the foot treads is what we possess.

In other words, you need to enter into it by the small and tiny things. Many of us are paralysed by the greatness of our dreams, the bigness of our vision. In some ways that's okay; it is good to have a big vision, but, in my experience, having a big vision really paralysed me.

We can be paralysed by the size and scope of God's promises but to *enter* into the fulfilment of them is *by the sole of the foot*. That is why we need to pay attention to what happens in the everyday and the ordinary. That is why we have to follow our hearts in the small things. That's why we have to pay attention to the tiny desires because if you let those tiny decisions of your heart slip and don't pay attention to them and don't act on them you will remain forever paralysed by the bigness of the dream.

Some of us are completely overwhelmed by our vision of what we want our life to be like. Some may even be suffering depression because there is a credibility gap between what we perceive our dreams to be and the life that we are actually living. Satan has a real part in helping to keep this credibility gap open but I believe that as we begin to realise that entry into promises is by the sole of the foot, little by little and it even begins in the ordinary things.

You may have a dream, a genuine God-given promise to be a preacher or a speaker but if you're not satisfied to speak in front of five or ten people you will never enter into promise beyond that, because the speaking in front of ten people is to enter by the sole of the foot. You may have a dream to distribute a lot of money and to be given responsibility for huge amounts of money in the kingdom, but if you cannot do that with your 10 dollars you cannot enter into the bigger inheritance.

This is what Jesus meant by being faithful in the small things (Luke 16:10). It is the same as the sole of the foot. The small things are not to be bypassed. They are the entry into promise.

Look again at the sole of your foot. It is a very small area. Learn to enter in bit by tiny bit. To trust that such a small thing will lead to something more significant takes faith and courage. We are suspended in our wilderness experience because we do not recognise the potential of 'the sole of the foot.' We expect to be propelled dynamically into promise. If someone else were to do this for us it wouldn't require us to have any faith.

Some of the great preachers started off by going into the forest and preaching to birds and squirrels. I heard of a very significant preacher who went into a field and set railway spikes up in rows and preached to *them*…with anointing!

If you feel called to heal the sick why not pray for some animals? I have prayed for animals and seen them healed.

The sole of the foot can be mundane, ordinary and even boring.

The Pentecostal/Charismatic movement, during the last few decades, has generally focused on the spectacular and has underrated what is ordinary. We have missed the truth of entering in by the sole of the foot. When we don't appreciate the sole of the foot we are trapped in unfulfilled prophecy and unrealised promise.

If you don't have enough faith for something big, exercise your faith for something small. You only need enough faith for the next step, so place the sole of your foot in front of you and then rest your weight on it. Walking is a series of steps. You place one foot down then lift off from the previous position and propel yourself forward.

Confidence doesn't come to us in huge dollops. We gain confidence for new things bit by bit. Even though Israel had experienced the miraculous parting of the Red Sea, it doesn't mean they had automatic confidence to enter into the land.

You can witness a spectacular move of God but still miss out on your own inheritance because you are not willing to place the sole of your foot in the next unclaimed piece of spiritual ground.

So, to all of you people praying for revival; it may well come by the sole of the foot. Minister to the 'one,' let God look after the thousands.

You may have a calling to distribute billions of dollars in the Kingdom of God, but you need to begin with ten or twenty dollars.

It is fashionable to talk about what our dreams are, and I am not minimising that, but do not allow your dreams to swamp you in depression because you can never see the possibility of them being fulfilled. Sometimes we lose hope and think that God is doing everything *except* leading us into our God-given dream. Let me suggest to you, He may be leading you by the sole of the foot.

It is easy to confuse our human dreams and ideals with what is genuinely given by God. Some of our 'dreams' or 'visions' can be generated out of an orphan need to be significant. God has to deal with us so that we dream the dreams that He has for us, rather than wasting our lives following pipe dreams and fantasies.

A pastor was asking a young guy what sort of wife he desired to have. So the young guy described his ideal woman. The pastor's response was, "So what you are telling me is that you want to marry Mother Teresa in Claudia Schiffer's body?" The young man had an ideal to marry a stunning and godly woman who had an amazing heart of compassion. He had given a very detailed, but unrealistic, picture of an ideal. The *perfect* person for you is not the same as your *ideal* person.

Be careful about 'ideals.' God is not a God of the 'ideal.' I used to be extremely idealistic and then God spoke to me about it; He said, "Ideals are Idols." Hmmm… That was a wake-up call to me!

I know some people who cannot let go their sense of calling. The paradoxical thing is that you need to have a sense of calling, but that then needs to die before a true calling can be realised. Why? Because true callings only come by resurrection power.

Ask yourself what 'the sole of the foot' looks like for you? What is the next step? It is, most likely, a small step. Don't undermine it; it is the sole of the foot. If there is a little thing to do we need to do it. It may not seem spiritual but we need to follow it. All these little decisions are a movement into destiny by the sole of the foot.

CHAPTER SIXTEEN

Spying Out The Land

In Joshua 2:1, Joshua commissioned two spies to go into the land ahead of the main body of people. Their task was to spy out the potential of the land and assess the potential threats and opportunities. Spying out the land is an essential step before we actually enter into our promised inheritance. Spying is not obvious; it is undercover and subversive. In spying out the land of our inheritance we need to be subversive because it is easy for our God-given dreams and visions to be stolen away from us.

PERMISSION TO BE SUBVERSIVE

God's activities are not always obvious or easily recognised. God often works subversively. We may have circumstances that we find difficult and very stressful. We may even have heartbreaking circumstances or times of great emotional pressure. We may be in circumstances of real boredom, just getting on with the mundaneness and ordinariness and tedium of everyday life. The truth is that God is actually working in our life to spy out the land that He wants to lead us into.

Jesus Himself was subversive. He said to His disciples,

"I'm not going to go up to Jerusalem to the feast'" but when they went away He went up to the feast secretively. (John 7:10) Jesus also exhorted His disciples to be as "crafty as serpents and as harmless as doves." (Matthew 10:16)

If God is subversive we have permission to be subversive too. I am *not* talking about covering things up. I'm *not* talking about not being open and honest to people. I am saying, however, that it is possible for us to give Satan the runaround. Satan is actually quite predictable in the way he works. The Devil is very legalistic and very religious. He works by rules and systems and is not a lateral thinker. God was ultimately subversive when Jesus died on the cross. Satan thought he had won when the kingdom of God was reduced to a naked, battered man hanging helpless on a cross. Satan was caught off guard because the naked man was none other than the Lion of Judah who disarmed the principalities and powers and made an open show of them. (Colossians 2:15)

When you are making progress into the land of your inheritance you need to be subversive about it. Any vision that God gives you will require His supernatural help. If you are too blatant about what God has put on your heart, you will have all the naysayers and the cynics against you. You need to hide from them until such a time as God leads you. Some people put everything up on Facebook, all their struggles, all their hopes, all their dreams. By doing this, they then open themselves up to all sorts of advice, counsel, humour, even anger. I'm not against being open and honest but it can leave you exposed to things that you need to be protected from.

If you have a vision protect it until the time comes for it to be manifested. A pregnancy needs to be hidden and protected until the baby is born. If we poke at a cocoon to assist the caterpillar's process of transformation, we will kill it and the beautiful butterfly of promise will not emerge.

Do not be in any hurry to jump the gun and go into ministry. Some people sit under anointed preachers just to get sermon topics to preach themselves. If you are sitting under anointed revelation allow it to be inseminated into your spirit first and then you will become pregnant with it. Don't miscarry it by trying to preach it too soon. Be hidden, keep it under wraps until it is time to give birth to it.

In Christianity there is a time to be bold. I myself have spoken and shouted things from the rooftop. But there's also a time to be subversive, to be undercover, to spy out the land.

VIEWING THE LAND

"Go view the land" — JOSHUA 2:1

In order to enter into your inheritance you need to view the land. In other words, you need to be willing to try things out. What works for you and what doesn't work for you?

If you are afraid to make mistakes. If you only want "the perfect will of God" you are not actually willing to "view the land."

The perfect will of God is not some elusive ideal, or an impossible tightrope to balance on. On the contrary, the perfect will of God can only be discovered by being comfortable with imperfection. The perfect will of God is *not* perfection—it is grace!

The two spies viewed the land. They were looking at the landscape, assessing the topography, determining what areas would be good for various types of farming. What is defendable against attack, what are the opportunities and the challenges? They were sitting down and counting the cost.

Look into your heart. Examine your motives. Would you *really* want to have a high-profile international ministry? Could you really handle all that pressure? Would you really want to do what so and so is doing? Or would you rather allow God to mould you for the bespoke task suited to you? As Paul says:

> *"For we are his workmanship, created in Christ Jesus for good works, which God prepared beforehand, that we should walk in them."* — EPHESIANS 2:10

When you are under religious condemnation it is not

possible to view the land. You want God to spoon-feed your inheritance to you because you are afraid to ask for what you want. The inheritance was allotted to the people; it wasn't a free for all, but within that there was leeway for people to ask for what they wanted. Reading through the book of Joshua we see the faith and boldness of some individuals when it comes to appropriating what is promised to them.

In Joshua 14, we see Caleb, at eighty-five years of age, (who had been one of the spies sent out from Kadesh-barnea and who had brought a positive report of the Promised Land) and he comes to Joshua and says:

> *"And now, behold, I am this day eighty-five years old. I am still as strong today as I was in the day that Moses sent me; my strength now is as my strength was then, for war and for going and coming. So now give me this hill country…"* — JOSHUA 14:10-12

In Joshua 15:18-19, Caleb's daughter boldly approached her father (the great inheritor undeterred by age). As a daughter she boldly asked him for the springs of water as well as the Negev, which was hers already, and he gave her the upper springs and the lower springs. She was confident enough to know what she wanted and she received it.

In Joshua 17:3-6, there is a man called Zelophehad and he had no male offspring. In the culture of that day the inheritance only went to males. Zelophehad had five daughters.The daughters of Zelophehad were undeterred by their apparent disadvantage. They boldly approached Joshua and Eleazar the high priest and asked for an inheritance equal to that of the men. They saw the heart of the Lord in rewarding the boldness of faith in spite of the obstacles.

In servant-hearted Christianity we are terrified of getting it wrong. We are paralysed waiting for the command of God and the perfect will of God. In sonship, making a mistake or getting it wrong isn't a problem, because you know that the Father loves you. He will correct the mistakes and use your mistakes to teach you. In fact, mistakes are a perfect learning opportunity.

My children make mistakes, not because they are rebellious, but because they are exploring and experimenting with *life*. Making mistakes is part of growth. The more willing you are to take risks and follow your heart, even if it means getting things wrong sometimes, the more you will experience God actively parenting you.

In sonship you can try things out to see what does and what doesn't suit you. There is no condemnation to those who are in Christ Jesus (Romans 1:1). The law of sin and death is a law of fear, of holding back, and of perfectionism. The law of the Spirit of life is an exuberant river, bubbling and babbling within the banks of the loving fatherhood of God.

This is a very different way of living to how we have

been conditioned to live as servants. In servanthood we are paralysed until we can know the 'perfect will' of God. But the perfect will of God is not a tightrope; it is a wide open meadow, an expanse which can be explored. Do you really want to know what the perfect will of God is? The perfect will of God is to receive the Father's love and to be transformed by it. The perfect will of God is that we become like His Son. The perfect will of God is that we become manifestations of love. When you are walking in love you have increasing freedom. You are only truly free when you become Love because the love of God can do no wrong.

The Tree of Knowledge wants to lock us into its definition of 'excellence,' which means to be flawless and perfect. But God's excellence is not like this. Excellence in life is very messy! Look at a piece of art. Its creation is messy and oftentimes it looks messy close up, but stand back from it and it is beautiful. Or consider a little child. A baby is excellent, yet messy. A toddler learning to eat solids is really, really messy but it is *excellent*. The most anointed worship I have been in has been messy, not what many view as 'excellent' but the Holy Spirit obviously loved it and showed His pleasure by manifesting a glory-heavy atmosphere.

A healthy child has an inbuilt need to run freely and explore widely. It is the responsibility of the adults to assess risks and to keep them safe. I encourage you to let Holy Spirit assess the risks. Explore freely; you will know when He shuts the door or tells you to get down from a height in case you fall. Abandon yourself with joy to the active parenting of your heavenly Father.

When my son, Jacob, was 3 years old, I bought him a new bicycle. He wanted a red one so that is what he got. I put the training wheels on it and got him pedalling. He grew in confidence daily and, within a week, he was merrily riding up our long driveway towards the road. Full of the joy and freedom of exploration, he had no clue of the dangers of the road. But whose responsibility was it to close the driveway gates? Certainly not his! It was *my* responsibility to close the gates and keep him safe.

Get on your little red bike and start pedalling! Father will close the gates for you if you are getting near danger. As His child you are free to explore and then experience Father caring for you. In the love of the Father, it is not (at least, in the beginning) our responsibility to manage our own behaviour. It is enough to stay in His love.

This is exactly what the apostle Paul and his team experienced when they were travelling:

> *"And they went through the region of Phrygia and Galatia, having been forbidden by the Holy Spirit to speak the word in Asia. And when they had come up to Mysia, they attempted to go into Bithynia, but the Spirit of Jesus did not allow them. So, passing by Mysia, they went down to Troas. And a*

vision appeared to Paul in the night: a man of Macedonia was standing there, urging him and saying, "Come over to Macedonia and help us." And when Paul had seen the vision, immediately we sought to go on into Macedonia, concluding that God had called us to preach the gospel to them."
— Acts 16:6-10

They attempted to go to Bithynia but the Spirit of Jesus did not allow them. Paul got on his 'little red bike' and started pedalling toward Bithynia. For some reason it was not the best thing to do at that time, so Father closed the driveway gates and sent him to Macedonia instead.

Paul didn't wait to "hear from God" about whether he should go to Bithynia or not. He went and when it didn't work out he adjusted his course according to what was then revealed to him. Hearing from God is different in sonship than it is in servanthood. God is not ultimately interested in giving rote commands to His sons and daughters. He wants to walk in relationship with them.

The more childlike you become, the more you will experience the nuanced and intentional care of the Father. He will close off one way, then show you another way. He will take away food that will make your tummy sore, and then feed you with food that is good for you. He will lay you down for a nap, then play with you another time. You will experience His love and His affirmation, and only on that foundation, will you accept His loving discipline. Whenever I discipline my daughter, she instinctively falls *into* my arms, not away from them. She feels *more* loved, not less loved, when I discipline her. We need a foundation of love to receive and recognise the Father's discipline.

I want to recommend my little book *Creating a Shape for Life to Flow*. It helps us to begin to view the land of our inheritance. It helps us to create the individual shape of our sonship by saying, 'No' to false obligations and then to take baby steps into promise by saying 'Yes' to the desires of our renewed heart. Saying 'No' to what is not on your heart and 'Yes' to what is on your heart is 'viewing the land.'

Fear not. You may feel as if you are too old (Caleb didn't let that stop him) or (like Zelophehad's daughters in Joshua 17) that the odds are stacked against you. As you become free of judgment against yourself and others, however, you will begin to see possibilities that you didn't see before. You will also experience faith rising within you to help you receive the desire of your heart. Ask for the inheritance that He delights to give you!

Rahab The Prostitute

The two spies arrive at the house of a woman named Rahab:

> *"And they went and came into the house of a prostitute whose name was Rahab and lodged there."* — JOSHUA 2:1

Now that's absolutely remarkable! A key person in facilitating the entry into the land of promise was a prostitute. She wasn't a converted prostitute or a 'saved' and 'born again prostitute.' She was still working as a prostitute, but God sent these two men to live in her house. Maybe she thought they were potential clients of hers. The amazing thing is that this prostitute Rahab actually became the great-grandmother of David. She was included in the Royal Messianic line of sonship, one of the ancestors of Jesus Himself (Matthew 1:5).

The question I wish to put to you is this:

Who is Rahab the prostitute in *your* life?

Who appears unsavoury to you?

What do you think God would *never* work through?

Scripture shows time and time again that God *does* use the unsavoury things, the foolish things, even the supposedly illegitimate things. God has to deal with our prejudices. God had to do it with Peter (in Acts 10) in order for the Holy Spirit to break through for the promise of God to come to the Gentiles. Peter was praying on the roof, fell into a trance and the great sheet came filled with disgusting, vile and un-kosher things which he was commanded to eat.

There may be a Rahab who is going to help you to get into your promise. I don't know who or what that is, but you may have a prejudice about something you think that God could never use. But God wants to lead us through those things into the promise and the inheritance that He has prepared for us.

Rahab had spiritual discernment and she perceived that God had given them the land. (Joshua 2:9) She hid them, then let them abseil down the wall from her house to evade capture, and hung a scarlet cord to identify her house to the Israelites when they entered the land. She may have had an immoral profession but it didn't stop God from using her to open up the inheritance.

Coming into our inheritance necessitates having the eyes of our hearts open to see things that otherwise we would not recognise. We can begin to enter promise when we recognise God in places where we are not looking for Him.

What do we have prejudices against? What have we

dismissed out of hand as being insignificant or worthless? What are we judging to be 'dodgy?' Look again at work, people, places and cultures. Jesus saw every person with the Father's eyes. Maybe you need to deal with a judgment in your heart against that which is mundane and ordinary. Maybe you have a culturally defined view of what ministry is and you cannot see beyond that. Maybe you have a pet doctrine that you are not willing to let go of. Our pre-judgments act as a cataract in our eye that stops us seeing the promise.

I can really identify with this. I have a 'doctorate' in judgment. I was always assessing what God could use and what He couldn't use. That prejudice has been eroded over many years of being humbled, and with the love of God coming into my heart. I remember praying for someone for healing. I and another guy were ministering and I prayed what seemed to me to be a very authoritative and prophetic prayer. The person still had pain. Then my praying partner spoke (and I judged his prayer as being 'wimpish' and a bit silly) but the pain immediately left the person. I was certainly left with egg on my face but God did His work.

I worked in full-time employment from age 17 to age 46 before entering into 'full-time ministry.' Looking back on it, God was preparing me *but it also had tremendous value in itself.* Sometimes we can get frustrated with the seeming mundaneness in everyday life because we cannot see that we are *already* being divinely favoured in our work life as a teacher, a manager, a business owner. The kingdom is bigger than our current perceptions.

God does not recognise the splits that have been created by things like Greek philosophy and religion. God does not recognise any divisions between the sacred and the secular. God does not judge any person on the outward appearance; He looks on the heart. Obviously God saw Rahab's heart and had been working on Rahab's heart for years before the spies showed up at her house.

If you are deeply unhappy in your job, yes, do look for something more suited to you. But if you love your work and you feel God's favour in it, and there is anointing flowing through it, don't hanker after 'ministry.' Take another look; ask for the eyes of your heart to be opened to see God in it, to see that you can walk in anointing in that area.

A working prostitute facilitated the entry into the promised land. Imagine if a church got a word from God to take a particular city, but they had to go through a girl working on the street to get the breakthrough. Imagine the pastors allowing her to take the initiative and tell them what she could see the Lord doing. Imagine the church leaders submitting to the fact that a prostitute had the divine strategy to take the city. I love to imagine scenarios like this, the things that will happen as we grow in our understanding of the ways of God.

God's choice of Rahab is so typical of who He is. Why?

Because God uses the foolish things to shame the wise. (1 Corinthians 1:27) God confounds the arrogant. He chose "what is low and despised in the world, even things that are not, to bring to nothing things that are." (1 Corinthians 1:28)

Look again at your life. Is your entry into promise being thwarted or has it somehow ground to a halt? Maybe there is a 'prostitute' (or some similar 'foolish' thing) which you have dismissed out of hand. Look again. Maybe it is an ally to help you enter your destiny and your inheritance.

CHAPTER EIGHTEEN

Escaping From The Pursuers

When you begin to go towards your promised land, you will discover opposition. The orphan culture, within your own heart and all around you, will pursue you to try and stop you.

The book of Joshua tells us about the pursuers who were sent to hunt down these two men:

> *"And it was told to the king of Jericho, 'Behold, men of Israel have come here tonight to search out the land.' Then the king of Jericho sent to Rahab, saying 'Bring out the men who have come to you, who entered your house, for they have come to search out all the land."* — JOSHUA 2:2

Rahab helped them to escape these pursuers. She lied to the king of Jericho's representatives and hid the men under stalks of flax on the roof of her house. She knew that the spies were sent by Yahweh and helped them to evade and escape from their pursuers. In verse 22, it says that, "…they departed and went into the hills and remained there three days until the pursuers returned and the pursuers searched all along the way and found nothing."

When you want to enter into your inheritance and into your promise the 'king of Jericho,' who currently occupies your promise, will send pursuers after you to stop you doing that.

You won't get into the land of promise on a totally free ticket. This is why I'm having to write about this because the land is taken *by faith*. There are always those who are going to pursue us in our freedom. In Galatians, Paul is championing and contesting for the freedom of the Galatians who had reverted back into the Tree of Knowledge of Good and Evil. Paul says in Galatians 2: 4, "…yet because of false brothers secretly brought in, who slipped in to spy out our freedom that we have in Christ Jesus so that they might bring us into slavery."

The people about whom Paul wrote in Galatians are up to the same sort of tricks as these pursuers in Joshua. They are coming in to stop us moving into our freedom in Christ. Religion, in all its forms, spies out and pursues us to hinder us entering into promise. Legalism, both blatant and subtle, is pursuing us to spy out our freedom so that we would be brought back into slavery.

There are other things that are pursuing us. For example, historic and systemic misogyny acts as a pursuer to stop

God's daughters entering into destiny. There is a war against the expression of the intuitive heart, in women and men, trying to force our God-given creativity into a box. The pursuers try to fit square pegs into round holes. Pursuers are coming to try and spy out the freedom that God has given us to follow our hearts.

There are people who bring a form of Christianity that works purely from programme and formula. There is a style of leadership that seeks to overrule and lord it over us. These act as pursuers against our freedom, trying to stop us spying out the land of our promise and inheritance.

Rahab hid the spies. (Joshua 2:6) She was smart and knew what to do. If your authentic God-given expression is being pursued and harassed, you can hide for a while. Rahab's roof is a good place to hide. I am not talking about sin; I am talking about things that we may be prejudiced against. An ordinary job, normal life, is a good place to hide from the pursuers.

We need to develop the spiritual discipline of keeping our heads below the parapet. Too many Christians stick their heads up above the parapet and one of the enemy's snipers takes a pot shot at them. We are caught in the crosshairs of the Accuser's sights and he is able to pick us off. When David was being pursued by a jealous Saul he hid in the fields and was assisted by Saul's son Jonathan. (1 Samuel 20) When we are pursued we need to hide from the posse and escape from the hunters.

Get used to hiding in the bosom of the Father. You do not need to explain everything or even *anything*. If you are in a church where nobody understands you, don't try and make them understand you; just hide in the secret place inside yourself. If you cannot articulate what you have experienced, don't try to—just hide in the love of the Father for yourself. Enjoy that special love for *you*.

Jesus worked in the carpenter's shop until the Father sent him out to confront the demons. We cannot confront demons until we are sent by the Father. If power and authority is not working for you, go back to the carpenter's shop. Go back and work in hiddenness until the time comes for your sonship to be manifested. You are loved as much when you are sweeping the sawdust from the floor as you are when you heal the sick or cast out an evil spirit. Hide from the pursuers until they go away. There will be a time when you face the giants of the land but that is not now.

If you try to speak out everything before it is time to speak you will find yourself being pursued. Be careful about publicising your God-given dream too soon, because you will be pursued by nay-sayers and cynics. You will also be pursued by your own orphan fears and doubts. Hide your dreams in your heart; surround them in the Father's love. The day will come when they will emerge and will not be able to be denied. Allow yourself to be built up on the inside in a dark and comforting place.

Trying to understand the Bible by your own mind can be like being pursued. Our old theology pursues us to stop us entering into promise. We can get waylaid by problematic passages of Scripture. You can experience the Father's love and then be thrown because your natural mind tries to work out the meaning of a particular verse that seems to contradict another verse. My counsel is this: Hide in the experiencing of the love of God and *wait*. Hiding and waiting are spiritual practices which are vastly under-rated.

Soulish counsel can also be a pursuer against your inheritance. This can be negativity. You can have your hope stymied by a negative wet blanket thrown on your dreams. When I was taking a step of faith to follow the Holy Spirit to move from Northern Ireland to New Zealand a very well-meaning person sat me down and counselled me to settle down in Northern Ireland and remain there in a 'normal life.' This is not necessarily wrong as I have already said but it was not what God was doing. God was leading me to New Zealand.

Soulish advice is not always negative or cynical. It can equally be a pseudo-positivity, or an enthusiasm that is not inspired by the Spirit of God. You can be railroaded by forceful enthusiastic personalities when your heart is hesitating. You can easily be manipulated into doing things that your heart is not really in. I love it when sons and daughters learn to say, 'No!' When you are secure in your identity, it is easy to say, 'No' when there is a bigger 'Yes' burning inside us.

Negative people can spy out our liberty. Equally, enthusiastic people can spy out our liberty. The good is often the enemy of the best.

In highlighting the ways that Holy Spirit works, it is important to also highlight how the enemy works. Paul said we are not ignorant of Satan's devices. (2 Corinthians 2:11) The unfortunate truth is, we *have* been ignorant of the devices that Satan uses because we only focus on the 'bad' side of his personality and are oblivious to the deceptively 'good' side. If you become free from the knowledge of good and evil, you will certainly throw many pursuers off the scent!

Satan is not all bad, you know! He also has a 'good' side. Satan is pretty much synonymous with the Tree of the Knowledge of *good* and evil. He is the Accuser, making us feel guilty by measuring us against an unattainable standard. Always wanting to do 'good' and 'right' will stop you from experiencing favour and entering into the fulfilment of promise.

The two spies escaped the pursuers and they reported back to Joshua, "*Truly, the LORD has given the land into our hands and the inhabitants melt away*" — JOSHUA 2:24

CHAPTER NINETEEN

A Quantum Leap

"Joshua rose early in the morning and they set out from Shittim… and they came to the Jordan." — JOSHUA 3:1

You have spied out the land to see what your inheritance is. You now know that you can inherit one step at a time and enter in by the sole of the foot. You have successfully evaded those who pursue you.

Now something else is required. This is what held the children of Israel back and that is why many of them didn't enter into promise. They had to cross over the River Jordan.

This is huge! The day inevitably comes when we stand on the banks of the river. Our land which God has promised is so near but oh so far away. There is no alternative but to cross the rushing waters which foam and froth in front of us. Could we wade across? No, this barrier is too deep.

Taking a step of faith into the unknown is the scariest thing we are faced with. This is the deal-breaker. This is the difference between a transition period of eleven days or forty years!

We have to take a step into the unknown. We have to transition through a place of darkness and letting go. This is the letting go of all that we know to be familiar. In coming into who we are really meant to be, there is a chasm to be crossed. Taking this step is what ultimately determines whether or not we actually enter in or not.

This is what I call **a quantum leap through death**. It sounds scary and it is! But there is hope! I didn't realise this when I was faced with the death of everything I knew. Comfort-love helps us to step beyond what we can control and transition through the unknown. Leaving your comfort-zone doesn't mean that you are totally comfortless. When our kids start school they are leaving the comfort-zone of home but there is a residue of the substance of comfort in them to help them when they are in a new situation. The comfort of God will be there when you need it.

Death is unavoidable. As Christians we are dying to the false, orphan self, dying to an identity of servanthood. Repentance and laying down control involve a death. True forgiveness also involves a transition through the Jordan. Why? Because, we have every right, in the natural, to withhold forgiveness. To come to a place where you release your enemies, is to take a quantum leap of faith and pass through the Jordan.

Our lives are full of decisions that require risk, where there is no absolute guarantee of the desired outcome.

Progression in life involves a willingness to set off into the unknown. When a couple get married it is a venture into the unknown. When children are born the parents have to lay down their own agenda for the sake of their children. When you apply for a new job or receive a promotion you need to embrace the unknown in order to progress.

Every time I stand up and speak it takes a step of faith because there are no cast-iron guarantees that it will be a success. As a preacher, the distance between your chair and the pulpit can feel like a very long distance. Kathryn Kuhlman talked about being confronted with the door that she needed to open to come out onto the stage to preach. She felt afraid of that simple doorknob. It confronted her and terrified her. She counted the hours and minutes until she would have to go onto the platform to preach and she became fixated by the dreaded door handle to the stage. It was inexorable; the time would come when she needed to preach and she would have to grasp the handle of the door, turn it, open the door and step out in front of thousands of expectant people. A simple door handle represented Kathryn Kuhlman's River Jordan.

These things may seem insignificant to some but they are a crossing over the Jordan. The crazy and beautiful reality is that they are a catalyst for faith in the supernatural ability of God. I heard of a man who would receive a word from God before he spoke. Then the time grew shorter and shorter so that God would give him the message as he sat in his chair while the worship was happening. Then it shortened again, and the message would come to him as he was being introduced. Then he had to stand at the podium not knowing what he was going to say, but just open his mouth and start speaking and as he talked the message would be formed on his lips. That takes a real leap of faith through a kind of death.

Faith is spelt R-I-S-K. If you are creative, no one will ever know or enjoy your creativity unless you are willing to leave your comfort-zone and put your stuff in front of other people to really assess whether it is any good or not. Any writer or artist has to expose their craft to other people. That involves a death because their art is now before others to accept or reject.

Maybe you need to take a step into the unknown to believe for financial supply. If it's on your heart to go somewhere, to travel to a particular school or conference and you don't have the money for it, it takes faith to apply for it. Faith is always involved because there aren't any guarantees. The only guarantee is your experience of the faithfulness of God. Nothing is ever completely risk free.

In 2008, my 'Christianity' was finished but resurrection happened. After living my life in radical Evangelical Christianity, then radical Kingdom Christianity, I ended up hitting a wall. But I discovered something beyond death. On the other side of the river, the Father was waiting for me.

We have to leave the familiar behind to step into

something new. If you want to receive revelation don't be afraid to die to what you already know. If the Bible is death to you (2 Corinthians 3:6) lay it down so that it will return as resurrection life to you. In 2007, a prophetic lady told me that I would lose my understanding of the Bible. I knew a lot of Scripture and had a developed theological understanding, but her prophecy came true. Not long after she prophesied, the Bible became a closed book to me. I looked at it and it was only death to me. Then, two years later, it reopened in an unprecedented stream of revelation. Now, when I read the Bible explosions of revelation happen. I didn't look at the Bible for two years, then one day I opened it and the black letters transformed into a kaleidoscope of living revelation.

Our version of Christianity has told us, "Pray through," and "never give up." This is valid at some times, but at other times we are meant to surrender, to yield, to let go and to give up. Otherwise we will never experience life in another dimension, in the power of resurrection.

If you are in a crisis of faith, it may not be as big a tragedy as you think. Crises are very difficult when we are in them but they are meant to be a bridge to a richer revelation. When we come to a point where there is no option but to give up and let go, we will not lose everything as we fear, but we will transition through death to resurrection life.

The people are commanded to watch out for the ark of the

covenant being carried by the Levitical priests and then set out and follow some distance behind it. (Joshua 3:3,4) They have had no experience of this before but they will experience the Lord doing wonders among them. (Joshua 2:4,5) In entering into the land the wonders of the Lord are not external to them as they were at the Red Sea; they are *among* them. This is a significant difference from the exodus and is well worth paying attention to.

To enter into promise we must leave the status quo behind. We need to leave what currently feels comfortable to go to the other side. But real comfort abides in us and it helps us to move out of the comfort zone of the familiar. In going through death, we will discover that God lives on the other side—in resurrection. The Father is waiting for you on the other side of the passage through the birth channel. He will catch you in His arms as you emerge, He will rejoice over you, and He will name you with your true identity.

CHAPTER TWENTY

Priests Who Carry The Ark

Joshua recognised that the presence of God had to lead. The presence of God had led them out of Egypt and right through the wilderness. But it is in a different mode now. It is no longer the pillar of cloud and fire. No! The presence of God is now carried by priest-sons!

> *"And Joshua said to the priests, 'Take up the ark of the covenant and pass on before the people.' So the priests took up the ark of the covenant…"* — JOSHUA 3:6

It was the priests bearing the Ark who went through first. They went and stood in the Jordan and everyone followed them. In the New Covenant *everyone* is a priest *and* an ark. Everyone is a carrier of God's presence and when you realise this, you no longer feel the need to measure up to some sort of religious standard to be a carrier of God's presence. You are already chosen to carry the Spirit of God inside you. The knowledge of that alone should cause it to become more obvious to you and to others.

The New Covenant of sonship has made *you* a priest. (1 Peter 2:5,9) Then you can stand in the middle of death and you will find that the waters will roll back and that you will cross over to the other side and begin to take your inheritance.

When they came out of Egypt during the Exodus who went ahead of them into the Red Sea? Moses! The children of Israel only had to have enough faith to believe in their saviour (Moses) because it was *Moses* who put a staff into the Red Sea and it opened up.

Here in Joshua, however, something different happens. In order to go into Jordan, it is the *priests* who lead the people forward. The priests, carrying the ark, stand in the Jordan bearing the Ark of the Covenant.

This is super-significant in terms of entering into our inheritance. Let me put it this way: Until you and I realise that we are a bearer, a carrier, of the incarnated presence of God we will not be able to enter into inheritance. In order to enter into promise you have to realise that you are a priest yourself; that you are one who within your human person-ality, within your soul, your emotions, and your body, who carry the Ark of the Covenant.

You will need to be convinced by the Holy Spirit, without any doubts, that you, with all your weaknesses, failures, problems, your lack of success at living the Christian life, truly incarnate and carry within yourself the presence of God. Paul said that Christ *in you* is the hope of glory. (Colossians 1:27)

You will not be able to enter in and cross over into your promise if you think that the preacher or the pastor has a monopoly on the presence of God. You have to come to the realisation that *you yourself* are a priest; that, whenever you go through situations, when you take a leap of faith, even when you go through crisis, that you are a carrier of the presence of God. You realise that you can go into the middle of the Jordan and stand in that place, knowing that Christ lives within you. Then you will find that the waters will roll back.

Now, let me just say this prophetically:

The Ark of the Covenant was built in the wilderness. The purpose of the wilderness is so that we become incarnational carriers of God's presence.

When you find yourself going round and round in the wilderness and you wonder why you are stuck there, it is for a reason. The purpose of being in the wilderness is so that you come to a place of building the Ark, of realising that *you* carry the presence of God.

There is a time in the spiritual life when the self and God need to be integrated. God wants to fully integrate Himself within our humanity. If this does not happen we will remain in spiritual immaturity. We enter our inheritance as God-filled humans.

The Joshua-style leadership of the future recognises incarnational spirituality. This is a leadership that has stepped off the pedestal and is on the same level or even beneath—to lift us into confidence to walk in promise. Joshua leaders are not primarily platform leaders or ministers on stage. Joshua leaders lead into the inheritance by giving *everyone* confidence that *all* carry the presence of God.

Entry into promise is a question of identifying the life of God and following that life—the life of God in your life. When you realise that you, in all of your ordinariness, are a carrier of the presence of God, you are ready to make inroads into your inheritance. But, until you believe that you are a priest and recognise that you are being built into the Ark of Indwelling Presence, you will remain in the wilderness. You will stay in the desert until the realisation grips you that Christ is in you, that you are a bearer of the Trinity itself. In your spirit, soul and body you carry the presence of the Spirit of life. We are designed to carry the fulness of God (Ephesians 3:19)

When you see the anointed presence in your own self, the waters will part as you walk through them. The waters part for this specific reason. They part because you realise that what you carry on the inside is more powerful than anything else externally. That He who is within you is greater than he who is in the world (1 John 4:4). Then you can love the prostitute. When you are filled with love, the waters part because love always gives permission. When you are filled with overflowing love, and when you become love, then you, like Jesus, can hang out with the rejected of society. If God puts it on your heart, you can befriend the drunkards and the renegades. You will not be drawn into their lifestyle. They will be touched by the love that is within you.

This is a mystery that was hidden from before the ages (Colossians 1:26) but sonship is revealing it. Sonship is revealing the anointing that flows from within us. Paul wrote about this and we love to quote *some* of his words:

> *"Now to him who is able to do far more abundantly above all that we can ask or think…"* — EPHESIANS 3:20

Is that your experience? I have to say for myself, that sometimes it is and many times it isn't. There is a credibility gap between this and what we actually experience.

Do you know why we often don't experience the 'far more abundantly?' Do you know why we are not surprised that God does *more than we can ask or think*? Because we don't finish the verse. It is *according to the power that works within us.*

As we begin to experience God *within*, not God *above*, we will begin to experience His power *inside* us. Abundant power is experienced in direct correlation to power working *within* us.

Orphan-hearted Christianity longs and waits for God to open the heavens and drop something through the ceiling. But the only way to access the over-abundant ability of God, beyond what we can verbalise or even conceive of, is not to look up. It is to look *within,* to recognise *that* power and then to align ourselves with it. It is not according to the power in the laying on of hands by the ministry team at an altar call. It is not according to the power which works outside of us; it is according to the power that works *inside* us.

The revelation currently being unveiled to the Body of Christ tells us who we are in God. But another revelation is coming hot on its heels—the revelation of who God is *in us.* To a large extent the Body of Christ does not get this next revelation, because the vast majority of Christians are still entwined in the knowledge of good and evil and we look at ourselves and think, "How the heck could God ever live within *me*?" The scandalous and amazing truth is that He does! And when we realise that God's Spirit is intermingled with our spirit, we are ready to experience the overabundance of more than we can ask or even think.

Stones Of Memorial

Once they had passed over the Jordan there is another directive from Joshua:

> *"Take twelve stones from here out of the midst of the Jordan, from the very place where the priests' feet stood firmly and bring them over with you and lay them down in the place where you lodge tonight."* — JOSHUA 4:3

Twelve stones were taken so that the people of Israel would remember how the Jordan was miraculously rolled back. Then, another twelve stones were taken and placed on the riverbed to be covered by the river. (Joshua 4:9)

Stones on the river bank. Stones in the river. What is all that about?

In 1998 I visited the island of Iona, reputed to be the cradle of Western Christianity. Irish monks went out from this tiny island and brought the Gospel to Europe and beyond. There is a tradition on the island. On a stony beach in St. Columba's Bay you take up two pebbles in your hand. One represents your past, your sins, failures, everything you carry as a burden. You throw that stone with all of your strength into the sea. You keep the other stone as a memorial and it represents the promises of God.

This practice on Iona is somewhat similar to what happened here in Joshua. One set of twelve stones were extracted from the Jordan riverbed. These twelve stones were carried forward as a memorial and reminder of how the waters had rolled back when they passed over the Jordan. The other set were placed into the river and hidden from view.

The two sets of stones mirror each other. There is one set of stones in death, the other set in resurrection.

Some things are buried in death. Some things emerge out of death into resurrection life.

The rolling back of the Jordan is a symbol of God banishing the fear of death. We do not enter in because we fear being submerged and lost in the swirling waters of the unknown. We are terrified of relinquishing one reality in order to pass to a new reality. If we do not know the love of God the terror is very real. I have experienced it. But what rolls the dark water back? It is the love of God:

> *"...for love is strong as death...Many waters cannot quench love, neither can the floods drown it."*— SONG OF SOLOMON 8:6,7

Jesus died on the cross to remove the fear of death from us. The Bible says that:

> *"…through death He might destroy the one who has the power of death, the devil, and deliver all those who through fear of death were subject to lifelong slavery."*
> — HEBREWS 2:14, 15

We remain in slavery to the lies of the Accuser because we are afraid to enter into death. The thing is, death is the way to *escape* from Satan! We fear death because we think it is the end but it is actually a beginning because what follows it is resurrection. Satan does not exist in resurrection life.

The stones taken out of the Jordan also speak of the *reintegration* of what has died. Yes, we have died with Christ but what has actually died is a false identity. The real God-created identity will emerge beyond death. Everything that is the authentic you will come out of death into resurrection.

For example, I may have a particular set of gifts or talents. Then a time comes when these have to die. The reason they have to die is that they are what I base my identity on. That is not how it is meant to be. My identity is meant to be based on the reality that I am a beloved child. So, the false identity needs to die. But when the true identity is resurrected, the gifts and talents that are part of me reappear, but they reappear in a healthy way, in resurrection life. To the onlooker, I look like the same person and indeed I am but there is a fundamental difference. My false orphan identity has died, and I emerge out of a death *as a son*.

Have you been through a 'death' experience? What has come out of that? What has 'survived' that rupture? Whatever it is, it is eternal because it is birthed out of death and sustained by resurrection life. Be careful that you do not dismiss things out of an overly religious motivation. Some people are so condemned that they have no confidence whatsoever in their own intuition or their own heart's desires. I heard Bill Johnson say once that too many Christians are still trying to crucify the resurrected life. That is a very astute observation. If you have been through death, what you carry now is resurrection life—no matter how ordinary it looks.

We need to take a risk and start to believe that our feelings, thoughts, intuitions and desires are now from God and *can be trusted*. If we know that we have surrendered everything to God, we can safely assume that God has accepted that, so what is in our heart after that surrender is consistent with resurrection life. That is the overriding reality. That does not mean to say that everything will be an unmitigated success and there will be no more problems. What it does mean is that it will be part of "all things working together for good." (Romans 8:28)

Now, you may ask, "But what about temptation? That's not resurrection life, is it?" Well, no, it's not! I know something of temptation myself. But, I'll tell you this: I am learning to tap into the resurrected 'Stephen Hill' who is like Christ, who is a son of the Father, and who has been justified and set apart! When I can connect with *that* reality, temptation doesn't hang around too long. It has no landing ground and it slides away.

If you are deeply established in your identity as a beloved one, then you can begin to confidently live out resurrection life.

Twelve stones were placed back into the Jordan river:

> *"And Joshua set up twelve stones in the midst of the Jordan, in the place where the feet of the priests bearing the ark of the covenant had stood; and they are there to this day."*
> — Joshua 4:9

The stones placed in the Jordan disappear forever from sight but everyone knows they are there. They represent our death with Christ. Contrary to what religion interprets this to mean, it is a very positive thing. My shame, my guilt, my orphanness has died with Christ. The person who cannot receive the promise of God is dead! The person who is unworthy has died with Christ! The person who is full of fear and shame has been crucified with Christ. The person who has no hope and no identity is submerged in the death of Christ.

The death of Christ has also drowned the ambition to become self-righteously good. The delusion that I can somehow obtain inheritance by my own efforts is dead. The self-generated Christianity that I lived in for so many years is placed on the bed of the Jordan. When we are in the land of promise and inheritance we know that stones from the land are buried in death. Our inheritance is not gained by our own merits; it is purely a gift of God.

Another important thing to mention here is this: Memorial is very important, because memory helps us go forward. We are to cherish memory, we are to practise remembrance, but it is not to hold us back. As we transition through the death that faith requires, we mourn the past and acknowledge that it is part of us but it is also swallowed up by the waters of Jordan. Memory is a dividing line between the old and the new. If you have nostalgic memories, venerate them but also use them as stepping stones into destiny.

When memories rise up they could also be a signal of something new coming. People who come close to death often report that their life flashes before them. If you are filled with memories of the past, it may be that you are about to cross over into promise. Maybe your past life is flashing before your eyes and you are flooded with memories of the past. Have hope, because you may be on the verge of breakthrough.

The stones tell us that something has been learned through experiences of death. Death has not had victory in our lives but has produced something new, something that is resurrected. Our life has gone into death, but new life has emerged. We are, with Jesus, on the other side of the river of death. The promised inheritance begins to open up to us in resurrection life.

No More Manna!

When we enter into the promised land, things are different. A new level of faith is required because there is a new environment. The things that we depended on in the wilderness are not available any more. There is no supernatural leading by the pillar of cloud and fire. Oftentimes we can long for a repetition of times past, when there were outpourings of the supernatural. We do not realise that there are manifestations which are intended for the wilderness, but they won't work in the land of promise. We need to have hope that when one level of Christian experience begins to wane, it is often *within the purposes of God*. God wants to transition us from glory to glory. The manifestations that accompany our current degree of glory are not suitable for the next degree of glory.

The supernatural provision of the manna stopped when they entered the inheritance:

> *"…the day after the Passover, on that very day they ate of the produce of the land, unleavened cakes and parched grain. And the manna ceased the day after they ate of the produce of the land and there was no longer*

*manna for the people of Israel but they ate of
the fruit of the land of Canaan that year."*
— Joshua 5:11

In the place of promise and inheritance there is no
manna available to eat. In the wilderness the main supply
of food was the manna. The manna was not very appetising
but they didn't have to work for it; they just went out and
picked it up every morning. It was supplied from heaven.
But when they came into the Promised Land there was a
different food supply. The trees were laden with fruit and
once they tasted the fruit, the supernatural provision of
God in the manna stopped and dried up.

This may surprise you but it is very possible to go hungry
in the land of promise. Once you have tasted the fruit of
sonship, the fruit of the promised land, if you try and go
back to the way of eating in the wilderness, *you will starve.*
If you don't act by faith and begin to walk in your promise
by faith there is no other option. If you are afraid to stretch
out your hand and pluck fruit from the tree and are still
hoping manna will drop from heaven, it isn't going to
happen. However, you are free to eat the fruit of the land;
you can actually go in faith and take it for yourself.

Some of you may feel as if God has stopped the manna;
God has stopped feeding you in a way you are accustomed
to. Let me suggest that maybe the source of your food has
changed. Maybe you have gone forward into the land of

promise and there is fruit hanging on the branches of the trees that you need to pick. Maybe there is wheat or corn in the fields that you need to go out and harvest.

Let me tell you this; in sonship you can break through the fear that makes you hesitate. We need to break through the fear that paralyses us, the fear of getting it wrong because **the land of promise is a wide and spacious place**. In your inheritance you have choices and options and they are *all* filled with God's blessing. Some fruits you may not like but you can leave them for someone else and then pick the fruit of another tree that you prefer. Once you begin to feed this way you have outgrown being spoon-fed.

Of course we are always fed by God; *of course* revelation always flows; *of course* we're always comforted, but I'm making another point. I'm making the point that you can begin to move in faith and try things out.

In sonship, you discover the purpose of God everywhere. There is not a division between the sacred and the secular, the Jew and Gentile, the male and the female. The will of God is not a narrow tightrope that we have to walk. The will of God is a wide place because the perfect love of God is established within your own heart. Do you know what the perfect will of God is? The perfect will of God is to be loved by the Father and to be transformed by that love into the likeness of His Son.

When you experience being continually loved by the

Father, then you will begin to move by your heart and move by love and you will find that the land of inheritance is something that is perfectly suited to who you really are.

That is what I mean by eating the fruits of the land. The manna was the same thing for all the people of Israel; it was bland and boring. It was given by God, yes, but it was the same no matter who ate it. But in the land, you can plant seeds. If you like apples you can plant apple trees; if you prefer oranges you can plant orange trees. You can begin to cultivate out of a heart of sonship something that is true to you and that is uniquely shaped for you.

The Futility Of Human Might And Power

In chapter 5 it says that the new generation who crossed over the Jordan were circumcised:

> "At that time the LORD said to Joshua, 'Make flint knives and circumcise the sons of Israel a second time. So Joshua made flint knives and circumcised the sons of Israel at Gibeath-haaraloth. And this is the reason why Joshua circumcised them: all the males of the people who came out of Egypt, all the men of war, had died in the wilderness… Though all the people who came out had been circumcised, yet all the people who were born on the way in the wilderness after they had come out of Egypt had not been circumcised."
> — JOSHUA 5:2-5

The men that entered into the land of promise had to be circumcised. Ouch! Painful indeed but it served a significant purpose. Born in the wilderness they had not had this done to them. Those who escaped from Egypt were circumcised but forty years had passed and they had died on the journey. Now the next generation needed the foreskin cut. Why?

Circumcision was an identifier. It was the sign of God's covenant with Abraham. It was a mark of being different to the norm, a sign that they belonged to Yahweh. When they were circumcised it reconnected them to the hope of promise; it reconnected them to their forefather, Abraham. When the men looked at their anatomy they knew right away who they were and what God had promised for them—a land that they could live in.

Circumcision connected them to their forefathers but they could not escape being circumcised themselves. The older generation's dealings with God cannot compensate for your need to be deeply worked on by God. God has no grandchildren; each one of us needs to be formed in our own relationship with God. We cannot depend on the fact that our spiritual forefathers were circumcised. If we are going to defeat our enemies we need to be circumcised too.

Entering into the purposes of God is inextricably linked with knowing our identity as children of promise. We, Gentiles as well as Jews, are the offspring of Abraham. (Galatians 3:7) This is on the basis of faith and spiritual DNA, which is more authentic than biological DNA. Circumcision of the heart is a sign that we are mature sons of the Father.

In the New Testament Paul uses the metaphor of circumcision to describe a powerful spiritual reality. In Galatians, circumcision of the heart is what identifies us as sons of Abraham and co-heirs with Christ. If circumcision is a cutting of the flesh biologically, then circumcision of the heart is a cutting of the flesh spiritually.

This can be interpreted in a scary, religious way but it doesn't have to be like that. The truth is that we cannot enter the promises of God by our own performance. We enter in "not by might nor by power but by My Spirit." (Zechariah 4:6) The flesh, the old orphan identity that tries to prove something, to achieve something by our own effort or will, cannot enter into promise.

So when we have a crisis of faith it is actually a failure of might and power. Every struggle is the failure of your own might and power so that you can become 'in the Spirit' and receive the promised inheritance. Have you ever considered that your crisis of faith may actually be God circumcising your heart?

To be free of religious striving is a sign that you have gone through circumcision. What makes us religious has to be cut off because true Christianity is only by the Spirit.

Religion loves to tell us to cut off the flesh. But I want to turn the tables and say religion *is* the flesh. We can very readily get condemned by being 'bad.' But do we ever get condemned by being *good*? No, we don't, because condemnation sets the bad against the good. Good/bad dualism is the problem. Self-righteousness is as sinful as lust.

Circumcision, then, is the removal of the fig leaf. It is the removal of the stuff that we *think* makes us qualify. In truth, if you think you are disqualified, that is actually what qualifies you to receive everything from God! Jesus said, "The Spirit gives life; the flesh profits nothing." (John 6:63) That is not a religious statement; it is a statement of hope and liberation.

Circumcision is more, however, than just removing the fig leaf and being unashamed of our nakedness. It is a step *beyond* nakedness. Removing the fig leaf brings you to being your true self, but it *doesn't bring anointing.* Circumcision is a mark of God's anointing; it is life beyond death in resurrection.

You may be free of condemnation but still not entering promise. If you try to generate anointing by the power of your personality you need to be circumcised.

Circumcision is the removal of legitimate power in order to receive *spiritual* power. Our own strength is legitimate; it is not necessarily bad or sinful, but it *is* the power of the *soul.*

Circumcision is essential if we are going to be led by the Holy Spirit. Natural (soul-driven) personality traits need to be cut back to allow the Holy Spirit to be free to manifest Himself. This applies whether you are an introvert or an extrovert. As an introvert you have to resist shrinking back and being a wallflower. The natural tendency of an introvert is to repress their thoughts and refrain from speaking them out. They know what needs to be said but they do not speak it out. The Holy Spirit will push an introvert to sometimes break beyond their desire for aloneness or their penchant for repressing things, so that they can function properly within the Body of Christ.

Similarly, extroverts have to sometimes resist the tendency to dominate others. The tendency for an extrovert may be to talk for the sake of talking, and not listen to others. An extrovert can talk and talk without really saying anything of significance. God has created introverted and extroverted personalities and they both display Him. However, the Holy Spirit can also be hampered by the natural tendencies of both introversion and extroversion. Our personalities need to be circumcised so that we can be attuned to what Holy Spirit is doing.

When you are circumcised you realise, with a whoop of joy, that weakness is indeed the power of sonship. Supernatural power begins to operate when the flesh is impotent. You discover that Christianity works on the other side of failure and inability. It is truly, "…not by might, nor by power, but by My Spirit." (Zechariah 4:6) I really love how *The Living Bible* puts it; "My strength shows up best in weak people." (2 Corinthians 12:9)

In Joshua the army of Israel were circumcised in preparation for going into battle. Imagine that! Imagine that the main criteria for being a warrior is to be *circumcised*. But the foolishness of God is wiser than men and the weakness of God is stronger than men. (1 Corinthians 1:25) The enemy is wrongfooted by those who know they can do nothing of themselves but who have confidence that their God will show up.

When we are spiritually circumcised we lose confidence in our own ability to live the Christian life but we gain confidence in God's ability, *and* in our identity as the Father's sons and daughters. Natural circumcision applied to males only, but spiritual circumcision applies to both male and female. Spiritual circumcision cuts back those tendencies to live the Christian life by might and power, by sheer force of will and intentionality. Circumcision of the heart is a mark of sonship. Weakness *is* the power of sonship.

Where Is This Going?

This takes us up to the point of entry into the land. Entry into the land will look different for you than it will for someone else. Your experience of crossing over may not be exactly like your friend's experience of crossing over. And entering the inheritance does not mean that everything is smooth and downhill from now on. The Promised Land will present its own set of challenges. The walls of Jericho loom ahead and how will they fall in our lives? That is not for this book. What has been impressed upon my heart to share for *this* book is how to get from the wilderness experience across the Jordan and into the *beginnings* of fulfilment. I want to get you to a place where you won't go back, where you can only move forward, and where you see the fulfilment of prophetic promise over your life.

This is a summary of what I have written about:

Our destiny is hardwired into our humanity;

Entry happens differently than exodus;

Servants don't inherit; only sons inherit;

The promise is appropriated by the sole of the foot;

Don't be afraid to escape from the pursuers, to hide and be subversive;

Experiment your way into destiny.

I've talked about how God uses things which the religious mind finds offensive, like Rahab the prostitute.

I've talked about taking that quantum leap through the River Jordan through death by operating by faith.

Your inheritance is primarily *who you become*. I need to emphasise that to enter into promise and to receive inheritance is not primarily about circumstances and external things. The promised destiny is actually the transformation of the heart. It's not you or I doing or achieving something, although that will happen as an outcome. Primarily, it is you being transformed within your own heart to realise that Christ lives within you in all of your brokenness. Once you become changed within yourself, automatically things around you will be changed; and if they're not changed you will see them differently and you will begin to move in power and authority. Look for transformation of the heart first. Christlikeness is the destiny of every believer, and it will fill us with the Father's love. And what will a love-filled person do? It is impossible to quantify what they will do.

The tide of love is rising. The credibility gap between what the Bible says and what our experience has been, is inexorably closing. Let me take some of Paul's anointed words to show the direction we are heading in:

> *"For you did not receive the spirit of slavery*
> *to fall back into fear. But you have received*
> *the spirit of huiothesia (son-placing, not*
> *adoption) as sons by whom we cry 'Abba!*
> *Father!' The Spirit himself bears witness*
> *with our spirit that we are children of God."*
> — ROMANS 8:15

The Holy Spirit, within our spirits, is affirming to us that we belong to God, that we are His seed, that we have His DNA. Underneath all the doubt and the condemnation there is a cry of 'Abba, Father!' That cry comes from the Spirit who lives within *your* spirit. When you hear it you know that you belong to God:

> *"And if children, then heirs—heirs of God*
> *and co-heirs with Christ, provided we suffer*
> *with him in order that we may also be*
> *glorified with him"* — ROMANS 8:17

Our inheritance is nothing less than being co-heirs with Christ. Any suffering that we endure is part of the transition to receiving the same promise as Christ because we are co-heirs with Him. The mind boggles at this; the expansiveness of this is beyond comprehension but it is true.

I speak this as a prophetic word:

> *"For I consider that the sufferings of this*

> *present time are not worth comparing with
> the glory that is going to be revealed to us."*
> — ROMANS 8:18

My version (ESV) says that glory will be revealed "to us" but in the original Greek it says that glory is going to be revealed *IN* us. The glory will be revealed *within* us. That is a stupendous reality. The purpose of suffering is to prepare you and I as vessels to display divine glory.

> *"For the creation waits with eager longing
> for the revealing of the sons of God."*
> — ROMANS 8:19

Creation is longing for the sons of God. Creation itself is longing for you to come forth. Creation is not inanimate; creation is a living being and it is eagerly desiring us to come forth into our full identity. Creation is longing for someone to reverse the devastation in the forests and in the ocean. Do we know why creation is longing eagerly for the revealing of the sons of God? What will the sons of God do for creation? How will they help her?

In recent years it has impacted me that the Gospel is not limited to the human race. Humans are part (the most important part, doubtless, as they are the pinnacle of God's creation) of the redemptive plan, but God's purpose is to liberate the entire created order from bondage to sin and decay. That is as expansive as the universe which, by the way, is *still* expanding. The environment is certainly suffering under the Fall. Animals are subject to a lot of suffering and they suffer silently. Let us open our eyes and expand our hearts to align with the breadth of God's heart. Love will cause this to happen; don't resist it if it does. Don't resist a hunch or an urge to pray for creation. It may be a tree, you may feel silly, but you are participating in bringing the Gospel to all creation.

I prayed for a dog once and it was healed. I have also prayed for bees that have been drowning in our backyard swimming pool and they have made super-quick recoveries and flown away. I have a friend who has prayed for birds that have flown into his window and lay still for over an hour, and after him holding them on the palm of his hand and praying they have revived and flown away.

There is a beautiful story in the journal of Thomas Merton. One day he was sitting outside his hermitage at the monastery in Kentucky. In a daydream, he was gazing at the forest which was a few hundred metres away. As he looked, suddenly a deer came out of the forest. It was dragging its leg, which was horribly mangled, presumably from a hunter's trap. As Thomas Merton watched, a surge of compassion welled up inside him and he began to weep. As his tears flowed, suddenly the deer twitched and bounded off into the forest. It was completely healed! The compassion of God welled up in a man and reached across the clearing into the leg of a wounded deer. Creation will respond to love:

"For the creation was subjected to futility, not willingly but because of him who subjected it, in hope that the creation itself will be set free from its bondage to corruption and obtain the freedom of the glory of the children of God."
— Romans 8:20,21

God is going to lift creation up to the level of freedom of His sons and daughters. Creation didn't ask to be subjected to futility. Creation did not choose to participate in the Fall, but that has been its portion. God didn't design it for decay. Creation is designed to flourish under the dominion of love.

That is staggering! I don't know how to fully articulate what I am seeing, but creation is responsive to the love of God. If you have an orphaned heart, creation will remain orphaned. But if you have the heart of a son, creation is going to be responsive to you.

"For we know that the whole creation has been groaning together in the pains of childbirth until now." — Romans 8:22

Creation is pregnant; she is pregnant with the sons of God. This passage in Romans seems to suggest that creation is in contractions to bring forth children. There is a joining of heaven and earth. God will send the sons but creation will give birth to them.

The first Adam was made from the dust of the earth; the

second Adam came out of heaven and He was a prototype of the many sons. He was firstborn among many brethren, firstborn from among the dead. The sons of God are the offspring of heaven *and* earth.

The Spirit hovered over our chaos and something came forth. God hovered over the inanimate body of Adam formed from clay and he became a living soul.

Paul continues:

> *"And not only the creation but we ourselves, who have the firstfruits of the Spirit, groan inwardly as we are waiting eagerly for adoption, the redemption of our bodies."*
> — Romans 8:23

Recently it has dawned on me how inextricably connected to creation we are. In a very real way, we have a oneness with creation. Paul understood this. Creation groans and we groan too. We have the *firstfruits* of the Spirit of sonship, but where will the main crop of the fruit of sonship be seen? It will be seen in creation! We groan with creation because we feel the same frustration and pain as creation.

> *"For in this hope we were saved."*
> — Romans 8:24

We have received the Spirit of sonship so that we can give hope to creation. We can communicate the hope of redemption to creation. Creation can see the firstfruits of freedom in us and have hope that she, too, will be liberated. Our salvation is ultimately for the liberation of creation. We, like Joshua, will lead creation into promise and inheritance. This is heady stuff but it can be practised in your garden, while you are taking a walk, or wherever you find yourself in everyday life.

I want to impart a spiritual gift to you as you read this book. There is massive hope if we can see it. When it comes to entering into destiny we need a revelation of who we are in Christ. *This* is who we are. God recognises it. Creation recognises it. Do you recognise it? The Lord is doing something today which is unprecedented in history:

> *"Look! I am doing a new thing;*
>   *now it springs forth, do you not perceive it?*
> *I will make a way in the wilderness*
>   *and rivers in the desert."*
> — Isaiah 43:19

Do you perceive it? I hope what I have written helps us begin to perceive what is springing forth.

Inheritance is a gift. We do not work for inheritance…but we need to possess it. If we don't possess it we won't enjoy it. The gifts of God need to be unwrapped. It is imperative that the Body of Christ moves beyond the wilderness and into her inheritance. The only hope for a broken and hurting universe is for the substance of divine love to touch what is fallen and restore it to relationship with the One who loves it. God has chosen His sons and daughters, in the power of the Spirit, to be the ones who convey this amazing reality.

OTHER TITLES BY STEPHEN HILL

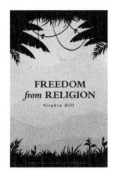

FREEDOM FROM RELIGION

Available at:
www.ancientfuture.co.nz

CREATING A SHAPE
For Life to Flow

Available at:
www.ancientfuture.co.nz

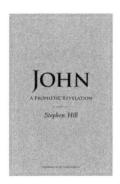

JOHN
A Prophetic Revelation

Available at:
www.ancientfuture.co.nz

Printed in Great Britain
by Amazon

16512028R00099